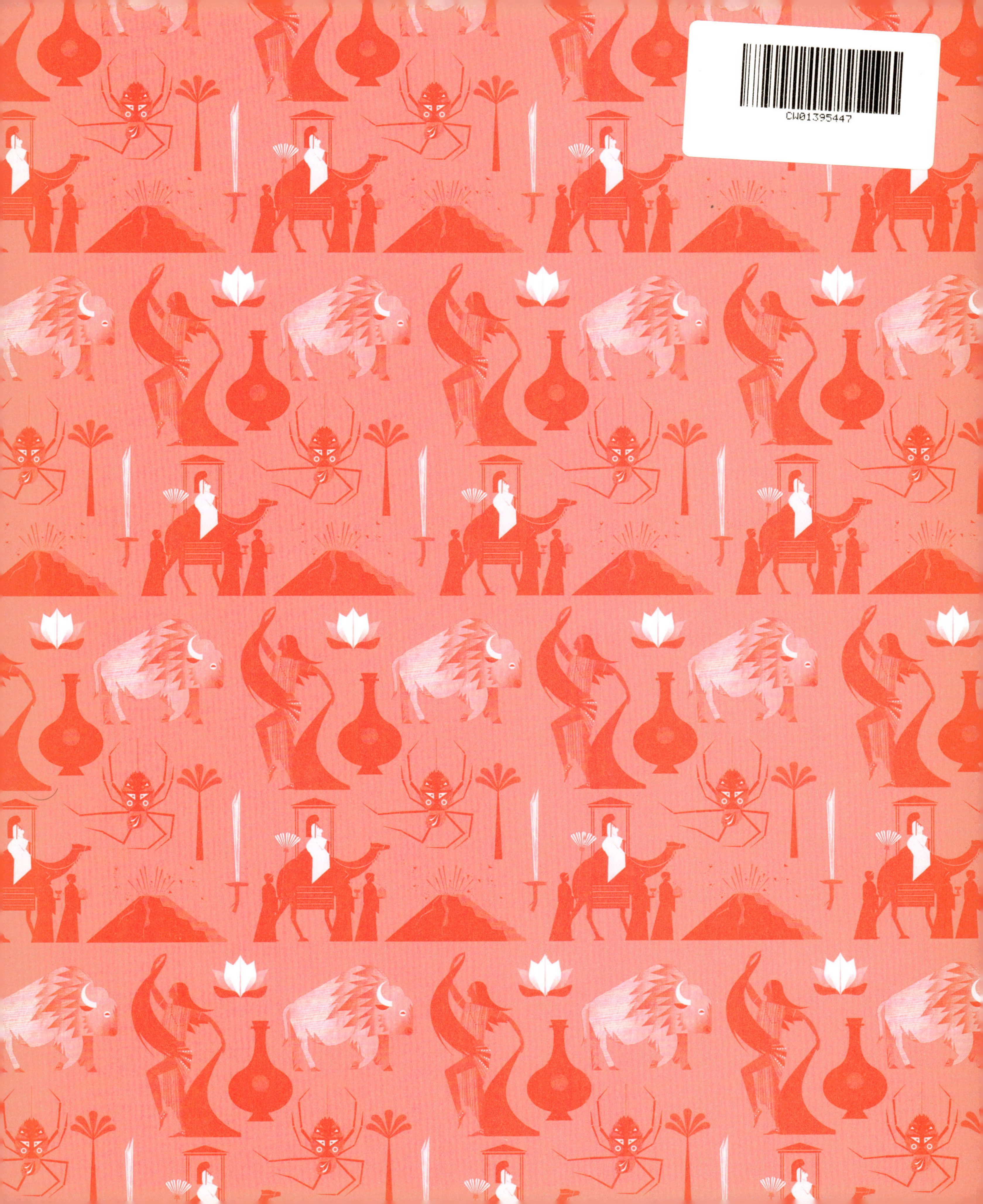

GODDESSES & HEROINES

WRITTEN BY JEAN MENZIES

DK

ILLUSTRATED BY KATIE PONDER

CONTENTS

MORTALS

ABOUT THE MYTHS

A note for readers

Each story in this book is just one version of many that exist. Different cultures, religions, and people may view the same events in different ways. Some of these stories are sacred and reflect the beliefs of people in the past and present. The tales of goddesses and heroines have changed over time, but all are wondrous in their own way.

INTRODUCTION

From the islands of the Caribbean to the mountains of Japan, and from the glens of Scotland to the shores of New Zealand, wherever you are in the world, at whatever period in time, you are sure to meet some remarkable women in the stories of every culture. Whether they are witches or warriors, goddesses or queens, these women continue to leave their mark through the tales that are told about them.

Within the pages of this book lie a selection of these stories. For example, you will learn how mermaids can be found around the world, whereas some goddesses' domains are so rare that no other culture recognizes them. However, each woman holds a unique place in the culture from which she comes.

DR JEAN MENZIES, AUTHOR

GODDESSES

Goddesses have been worshipped throughout history for the important roles they play in the creation and running of the Universe. In many religions, goddesses are believed to have made the Earth itself and all the peoples of the world.

As you will discover in the pages that follow, however, goddesses hold many different roles. From ruling over the afterlife to protecting certain animals, these powerful deities watch over almost every aspect of life.

CREATOR GODDESSES

Many different religions have a creator or mother goddess. These goddesses are often associated with the Earth itself and are responsible for the creation of life.

PAPATŪĀNUKU

PRONUNCIATION: pa-pa-too-a-NOO-koo

CULTURE: Māori

GAIA

PRONUNCIATION: GEY-a

CULTURE: Ancient Greek

Papatūānuku is the mother goddess of the Māori people from New Zealand. She represents the Earth, and when she refused to be separated from her husband, Ranginui, god of the sky, their sons forced them apart.

Gaia is the goddess of the Earth in ancient Greek mythology. She came into existence from Chaos, the huge chasm of the Universe, and then gave birth to the first generation of gods, known as the Titans.

NÜWA

PRONUNCIATION:
NYOO-wa

CULTURE: Chinese

Nüwa is a mother goddess from China and is often shown with the body of a snake. She created the first humans out of clay because she was lonely.

SPIDER GRANDMOTHER

PRONUNCIATION:
-

CULTURE: Indigenous People of North America

Spider Grandmother is an important goddess for many Indigenous People of North America, including the Cherokee. She watches over humankind and can take the form of a spider.

WAWALAG SISTERS

PRONUNCIATION:
WA-wa-lag

CULTURE:
First Australians

In northern Australia, the Wawalag Sisters are two goddesses important to many First Australians. They were responsible for naming all the plants and animals.

9

Papatūānuku's sons

Papatūānuku was goddess of the Earth and Ranginui was god of the sky. They were very much in love and they lay so tightly entwined that only darkness existed between them.

Together, Papatūānuku and Ranginui had countless sons. Their sons, however, resented living in the eternal darkness brought on by their parents' embrace. All but one agreed it was time to separate the god and goddess from each other. "Mother, won't you send father away so that light can enter the world?" they asked.

"I love Ranginui too much to be parted from him," Papatūānuku replied, only holding onto him more tightly.

To the goddess's surprise, her sons had prepared for this response.

Papatūānuku watched as first Rongo-mā-tāne, god of cultivation, tried with all his might to push her apart from Ranginui. Despite how hard he struggled, though, he could not move his parents at all. Then she felt as Haumia-tikitiki, god of food, tried in vain to separate them. Next to attempt the task was Tūmatauenga, god of war, but he could not succeed either. As each child in turn gave up, Papatūānuku laughed. "You will never part your father and me," she declared.

Yet, another son was awaiting his turn: Tāne-mahuta, god of forests. To Papatūānuku's dismay, she felt as Tāne-mahuta

wriggled his way into
position between her and
Ranginui and began to shove and
push with every ounce of strength he
possessed. At first, it seemed he would
fail like his brothers, until he found himself
with his head resting on the body of
Papatūānuku and his feet pressed
against the bulk of Ranginui.

**With a gigantic stretch, he felt
the two deities begin to part.**

"Tāne-mahuta, my son, stop what you
are doing," Papatūānuku shrieked. "Why do
you harm your parents so?"

Tāne-mahuta did not stop though,
despite his mother's cries. With one final
thrust, he forced the god and goddess apart
and light streamed into the space that now
existed between their bodies.

From that day on, although
Papatūānuku missed Ranginui greatly,
she provided a home for their
children while Ranginui
watched over them
from far above.

Tāne-mahuta pushed and pushed to separate his parents.

11

Spider Grandmother's bowl

One day, Spider Grandmother joined a gathering of Earth's creatures to discuss a very serious problem facing their corner of the world. They had no light to see by.

Spider Grandmother spoke first, "Without light, everyone keeps bumping into each other!"

"There are those on the other side of the world who have more than enough light to see, but they are too greedy to share," replied Fox. "We could take some from them, but which one of us can manage it?"

Their first volunteer was Possum.

Possum was certain that he could hide a little of the light from the Sun in his bushy tail and bring it back with him. When he tried, however, the light burned too brightly and singed off all his fur. This is why the possum's tail is always hairless.

The next to try was Buzzard. He flew
across the world to steal a little sunshine, thinking
to carry it on his head. However, the heat was too much
for him as well, and the light burned through his feathers.
From that day, the buzzard has always been bald.

Finally, Spider Grandmother stepped up. First, she
took a lump of clay and sculpted it into a sturdy bowl.
Then she spun her web across the Earth until she reached
the tree from which the Sun had been hung. She was so
tiny that no one noticed her, and she scooped some light
from the Sun into her bowl.

Spider Grandmother then proceeded to follow the
threads of her web all the way back home.

When she returned, everyone celebrated. Not only
could they now enjoy the light of the Sun, but they could
also make fire. From that day on, the lives of the people
who lived in that part of the world were forever changed,
all thanks to Spider Grandmother.

The Wawalag Sisters' travels

**Long ago, there were two goddesses
known as the Wawalag Sisters. The younger
sister was called Boaliri, while the elder
was named Waimariwi.**

Together, the sisters were travelling across northern Australia with
their two dogs, visiting the various peoples and naming the different
plants and animals they found. Waimariwi was also heavily pregnant
with her first child. After days of walking, Waimariwi came to a stop,
groaning. She had gone into labour!

Boaliri rushed to help her sister, and soon Waimariwi gave birth to
a tiny, wailing baby. With their new child to care for, the sisters decided
to find a comfortable spot to settle down for the time being. The place
they chose had a deep waterhole for them to drink from and numerous
palm trees that would shelter them from the sun. Content, they laid out
their sleeping mats and set about making a fire to cook the meat they
had caught with the help of their dogs.

Before too long, however, something very strange happened.

The wallabies and snails they had been cooking suddenly rose
from the fire, alive once more. One by one, the animals fled the flames
and ran to the nearby waterhole, leaving the two goddesses staring
after them. "What is going on?" asked the startled Waimariwi,
clutching her baby close.

It was Boaliri who spotted the cause of the commotion. "A snake!" she shouted, pointing to the horizon. "It must have smelled the new baby. We must flee!"

But it was too late to run. The sky had grown murky as dark clouds gathered overhead and lightning flashed around them. The snake that approached was no ordinary serpent, but the great Rainbow Snake, Jolunggul. It was he who had summoned the storm.

Quickly, the two sisters carried the baby to the waterhole, where they washed the child thoroughly. They hoped that without the scent of the birth the snake would turn back. Jolunggul, however, was not to be put off and heavy rain began to fall.

When their first plan did not work, the sisters had to think of something else.

So, Boaliri and Waimariwi took it in turns to sing and dance the sacred songs of the goddess Kunapipi. These were the first performances of what would become important ceremonies in years to come.

The power of the sisters' music beat back the rain and clouds until the sky was clear again and Jolunggul was driven away. Exhausted, the pair finally fell asleep with the baby and their dogs. Little did they know, however, that Jolunggul had not gone

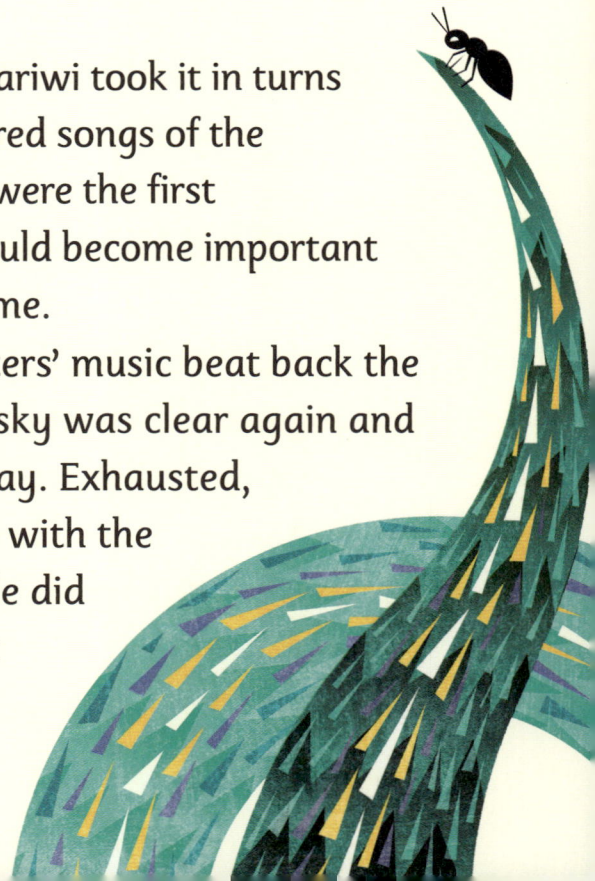

The pain of the ant's bite made Jolunggul vomit up the sisters, the baby, and their dogs.

far. While the sisters slept, the great serpent returned to their campsite and, before they knew what was happening, opened his massive jaws and swallowed all of them whole.

The sisters were trapped inside Jolunggul's stomach, but all was not lost. A tiny ant had been watching events unfold and, for reasons only it knew, it crawled up the serpent's long tail and bit down hard. The shock caused Jolunggul to throw up and so the whole group was released.

Jolunggul was still hungry though, and he opened his mouth once more.

This time, he swallowed only the two goddesses and then quickly slithered away. He went to join the other snakes, who all asked each other what they had eaten that day. When it was Jolunggul's turn, he tried to hide what he had done as he knew his companions would not approve of him eating the goddesses, but they kept asking. "Fine," he boldly declared. "I consumed the two Wawalag Sisters."

The other snakes were shocked, but they also knew that Jolunggul had made a big mistake. As they watched, he grew steadily more ill. "I can hold them no longer," Jolunngul proclaimed and for the second time he regurgitated the sisters from his stomach onto the ground.

Finally free, the goddesses returned to their child unharmed and took up their original journey. For Waimariwi and Boaliri still had much work to do.

GODDESSES OF DEATH AND THE AFTERLIFE

Every religion has its own beliefs about what happens after humans pass away. For some, this includes a realm ruled by a goddess of death who watches over the souls of the departed.

ATAEGINA

PRONUNCIATION: a-tai-GEE-na

CULTURE: Iberian

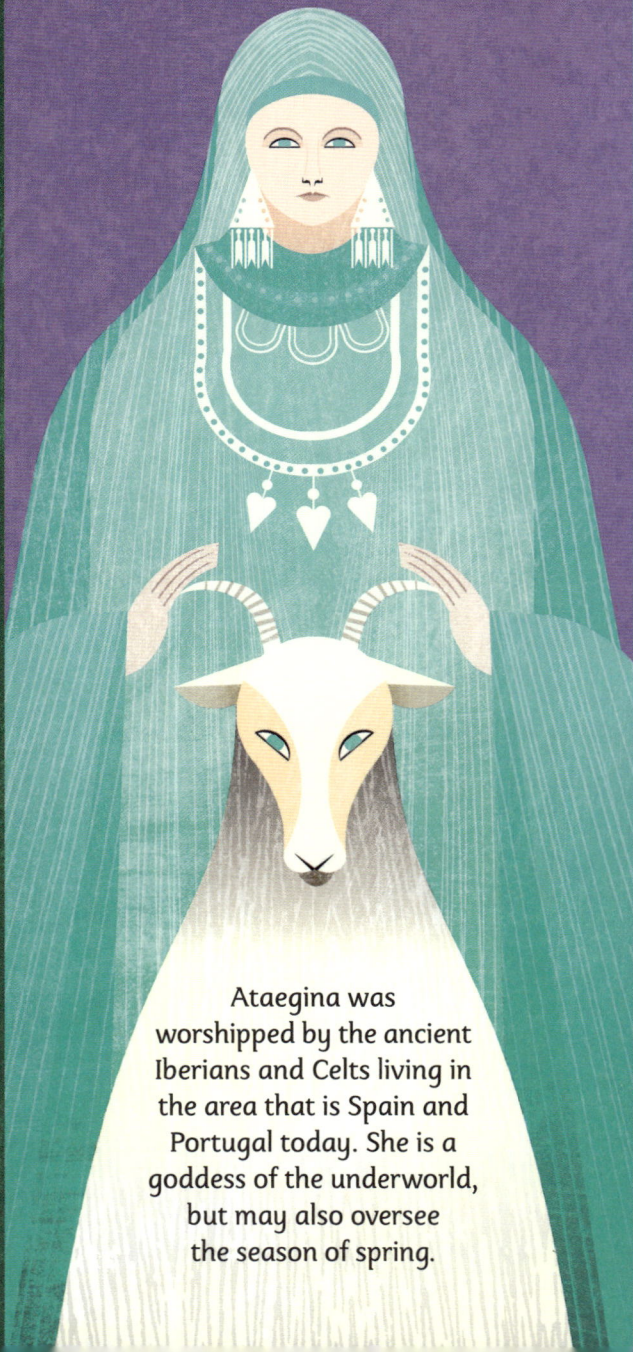

Ataegina was worshipped by the ancient Iberians and Celts living in the area that is Spain and Portugal today. She is a goddess of the underworld, but may also oversee the season of spring.

ITZPAPALOTL

PRONUNCIATION: ITS-pa-pa-lotl

CULTURE: Aztec

Itzpapalotl rules the Aztec paradise Tamoanchan, where humans were created and some people go after death. She takes the form of a skeleton warrior with butterfly wings covered in knives made from obsidian.

OYA

PRONUNCIATION: oi-YA

CULTURE: Yoruba

Oya is a Yoruba goddess known as an orisha. She is in charge of death and the afterlife, as well as being the goddess of the Niger River in West Africa.

MAMAN BRIGITTE

PRONUNCIATION: MA-mon BRI-jeet

CULTURE: Haitian

Maman Brigitte is a goddess known as a lwa in the Vodou religion of Haiti. She is married to another lwa, Baron Samedi, and together they are responsible for the dead.

TUONETAR

PRONUNCIATION: TOO-oh-neh-tar

CULTURE: Finnish

With her husband, Tuoni, Tuonetar rules over the Finnish underworld, known as Tuonela. She protects her realm fiercely and tries her hardest to stop anyone from leaving.

ISHARA

PRONUNCIATION: ish-AH-ra

CULTURE: Akkadian and Hurrian

Ishara was worshipped by different peoples, including the Akkadians of ancient Mesopotamia, as the goddess of many things. To the ancient Hurrian people, she was a scorpion goddess of death and disease.

ERESHKIGAL

PRONUNCIATION: eh-RESH-ki-gal

CULTURE: Akkadian and Sumerian

Ereshkigal rules over the underworld in the religions of the Akkadian and Sumerian empires of ancient Mesopotamia, found in modern-day Iraq. She is married to the god Nergal and her sister is the goddess Inanna.

19

Tuonetar's realm

Tuonetar ruled over Tuonela, the underworld, alongside her husband, Tuoni. One day, she was watching their daughter row her boat over the river.

The dark, rushing river separated the underworld from the land of the living. As her daughter approached, Tuonetar spotted a surprising passenger sitting beside her.

When the boat pulled up onshore, a man with long, white hair and a beard that reached his belly hopped out. This was the wizard Väinämöinen, and what was so surprising about him was that he was still alive. "Welcome to Tuonela," Tuonetar said. "You must have travelled far. Here, please accept this drink."

Väinämöinen took the golden goblet of beer the goddess offered him, but hesitated before he raised it to his lips. As he stared at the liquid, he saw that frogs, lizards, worms, and snakes writhed within. "I did not come here to drink poison," he declared, handing back the cup.

"Then why are you here?" demanded Tuonetar, dashing the cup on the ground.

"I seek three forgotten magic words that only those who have long since passed remember. I need them to finish building my ship in the land of the living," Väinämöinen replied calmly.

"Your craft will have to go unfinished, for no one leaves Tuonela," Tuonetar said in return.

Tuonetar then sang some magic words and the wizard fell into a heavy slumber.

While Väinämöinen slept, Tuonetar instructed her son to weave a fine copper net over the river to stop their guest from leaving, whether dead or alive.

When Väinämöinen awoke, however, he was not deterred, for he knew magic too. With a few whispered words he transformed into a tiny serpent. In his new form, he slipped through the holes in the net and swam across the river to safety once more.

Still, the wizard had learned his lesson and told everyone he met from then on never to risk a visit to Tuonela if they did not wish to stay.

Väinämöinen escaped through the net by transforming into a snake.

21

Ereshkigal's messenger

One day, Anu, king of the gods, decided to throw a lavish banquet for his fellow deities. He wanted to invite everyone, but unfortunately there was no way the goddess Ereshkigal could attend.

Ereshkigal was the ruler of the underworld and could not travel to the land of the living. So, instead, Anu invited Ereshkigal to send a messenger in her place, and the messenger was to bring back a gift. Ereshkigal decided to send her most valued advisor, the vizier Namtar.

When Namtar arrived at the banquet, he was greeted by the numerous gods and goddesses in attendance.

Each deity bowed in turn before the vizier to show their respect for Ereshkigal. All but one that was: the god Nergal. He considered Namtar too unimportant to receive his respect.

When Namtar returned, the goddess asked him how her fellow gods had treated him during his visit. "All were respectful except for one," Namtar told her.

"Who dared show my vizier disrespect?" Ereshkigal demanded. "I want them brought to me for punishment at once."

So, Namtar returned to the land of the living to fetch Nergal on the goddess's behalf, and they returned to the underworld together.

Nergal feared for his life. He expected the goddess of the dead to want revenge, so he prepared himself for a fight. When the doors to the throne room parted, he pounced and knocked the goddess to the ground. "Please don't kill me," Ereshkigal cried in surprise, her eyes meeting Nergal's.

At the sight of Ereshkigal's expression, Nergal found tears beginning to tumble down his cheeks. "I don't wish to die either," Nergal told her.

"Then let us call a truce instead. Marry me and keep me company in the underworld for six months of the year," Ereshkigal offered, as she was lonely ruling by herself.

A better offer Nergal could not have anticipated. The two soon wed, and lived happily together for half of each year.

Nergal knocked Ereshkigal to the floor.

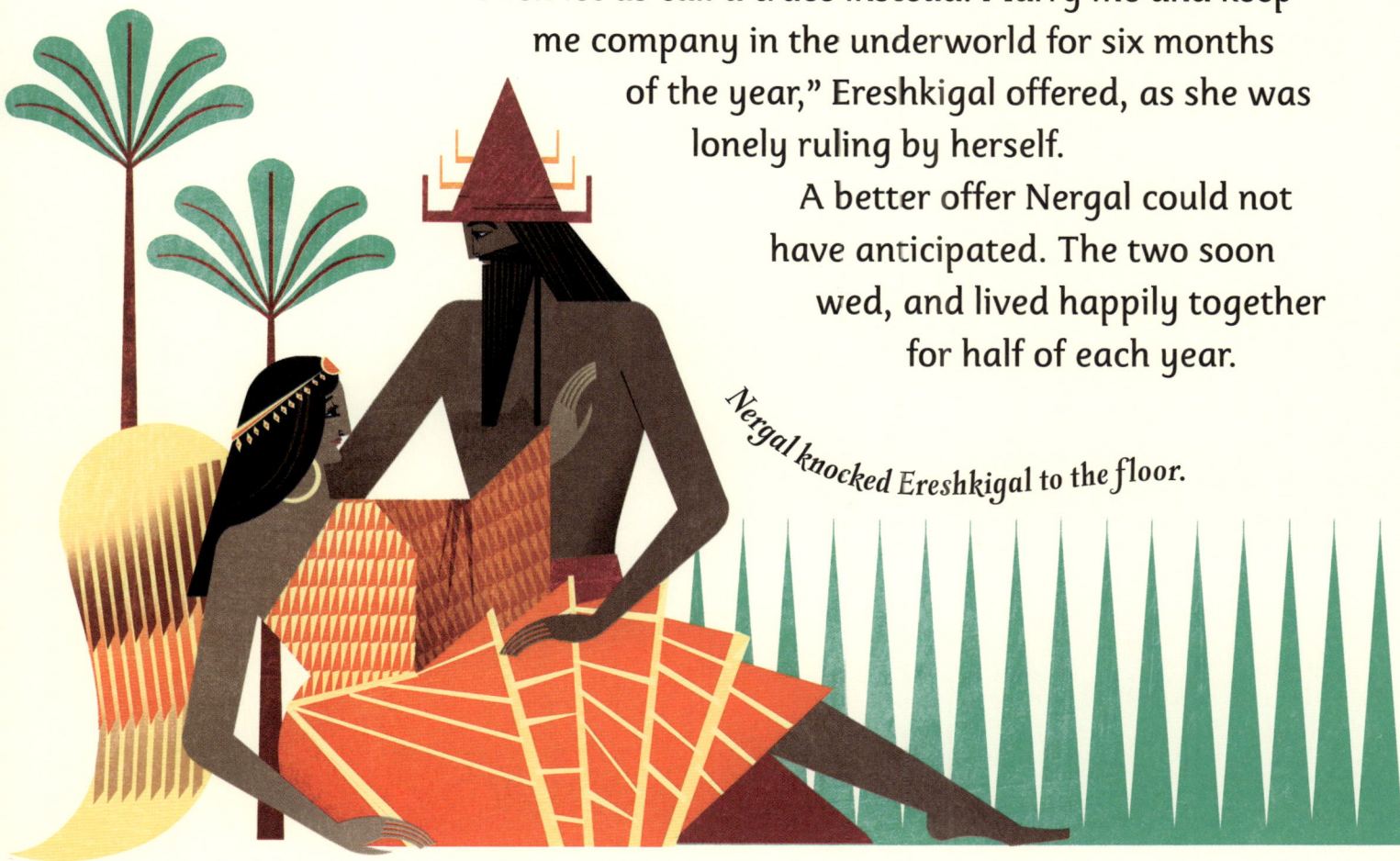

23

PRONUNCIATION:
SOW-lay

CULTURE:
Baltic

PRONUNCIATION:
a-ma-teh-RA-soo

CULTURE:
Japanese

Ame-no-Uzume is the goddess of dawn and the arts in the Shinto religion of Japan. She is particularly skilled in dancing and entertaining.

GODDESSES OF THE SUN, MOON, AND SKY

The days and months are determined by the cycles of the Sun and Moon. In many cultures, these movements are believed to be controlled by goddesses who travel across the sky.

Saule is the Baltic goddess of the Sun. She is married to the god of the Moon, Meness, and spends her nights asleep at the bottom of a lake.

Amaterasu is the goddess of the Sun in the Shinto religion of Japan. She is also considered one of the rulers of the heavens.

PRONUNCIATION:
A-may NO oo-ZOO-may

CULTURE: Japanese

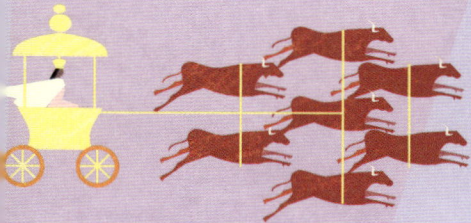

LUNA

PRONUNCIATION:
LOO-na

CULTURE:
Ancient
Roman

Ushas is a goddess of the dawn in Hinduism. She rides across the sky in a golden chariot and maintains order throughout the Universe.

Luna is the ancient Roman goddess of the Moon. Each night, once the Sun has set, she drives a chariot drawn by two horses or oxen across the sky.

Chang'e is a goddess of the Moon in China. She started life as a human, but drank a potion of immortality and was given a home in the sky.

Amaterasu's cave

Amaterasu was both the goddess of the Sun and the ruler of the heavens. She took her job very seriously and put a lot of effort into making sure everything in her realm ran smoothly.

Amaterasu's little brother, however, was a troublemaker. His name was Susanoo and he was the god of storms. Due to his wild behaviour, he was not allowed to rule over the world with his sister, but this only made him more determined to wreak havoc.

When Amaterasu divided up her rice fields, Susanoo broke down the fences she had constructed. When the rice was ready to harvest, he let horses trample her crops.

One day in particular, Susanoo decided to surprise his sister while she worked in her sacred weaving hall.

Susanoo hammered at the ceiling until a large hole appeared. Through it, he flung the body of a horse he had killed earlier that day. The horse landed on the ground beside Amaterasu, who leapt from her chair in alarm. In her haste, the goddess cut her hand on her loom. "This is the final straw!" yelled Amaterasu as she looked up to see her brother watching and laughing.

The goddess stormed from the hall to a nearby cave. She then pulled a stone across the mouth of the cave to lock herself inside. And so it was that the light of the Sun disappeared from the world.

Without Amaterasu, everything fell into darkness. Night and day were impossible to tell apart, and crops stopped growing. The rest of the gods and goddesses were furious at Susanoo. They were also desperate to get Amaterasu back, unable to bear the thought of living in the dark forever. So, they came up with a plan.

First, the gods gathered countless jewels and strung them from the tree that stood outside Amaterasu's cave. Then, from the tree's branches, they hung a huge mirror. Finally, Ame-no-Uzume, goddess of the dawn, lit a crackling fire and began to dance beside the tree. She sang and chanted, entertaining the rest of the gods so they laughed and clapped loudly.

The gods were so noisy that Amaterasu could hear them deep within her cave.

"What could possibly make the rest of them so happy when I have taken light from the world?" Amaterasu asked herself. Overcome by curiosity, she slid the stone door to her cave open just a crack and peeked outside. She was surprised to see her own reflection peering back at her from the mirror, while the Sun's light glittered on the jewels, dazzling her. The other deities quickly took the opportunity to grab her hand and pull her from the cave.

Now that Amaterasu was face to face with the rest of the gods, they begged and pleaded with her not to return to the cave. "We need you here with us, Amaterasu," they assured her. "Susanoo will be punished."

It was decided that Susanoo should give up the next thousand sacrifices made to him by the mortals down on Earth, and that they would be given to Amaterasu instead. The goddess was appeased by this and so she agreed to leave the cave, returning light to the world.

Ame-no-Uzume danced wildly, making the other gods laugh loudly.

29

Chang'e's elixir

There once lived a woman named Chang'e who was married to an expert archer named Yi. All was well until one day when ten suns rose in the sky.

The scorching heat from the suns was so unbearable that it threatened to be the end of all life. Someone had to do something!

It was Yi who took on the challenge. He grabbed his bow and went out into the warmth. Then he took careful aim and released an arrow.

Yi took aim at the ten suns and one by one shot nine of them out of the sky.

The arrow knocked one of the suns straight out of the sky.

Yi shot down a further eight of the suns, leaving only one behind. The remaining sun provided just enough heat and light on Earth. Impressed by Yi's skills, the goddess Xiwangmu decided to reward him with a priceless gift: the elixir of immortality, which would make Yi a god and let him live forever.

There was only one thing Yi truly loved, however, and that was Chang'e. If he were to become immortal, he would have to leave his wife behind, and this was something he refused to do. So, together Yi and Chang'e hid the elixir and carried on their life together.

Chang'e and Yi were not the only ones who knew about the potion, however.

Yi's apprentice, Fengmeng, had seen Yi receive the elixir and he was a greedy man who wanted the goddess's gift for himself. He waited until Yi was out hunting one day and then jumped out at Chang'e. "Give me the elixir," he demanded, threatening her with violence if she did not hand it over. Chang'e knew what kind of man Fengmeng was though and how disastrous it would be if he was granted immortality. There was only one thing to be done.

Chang'e grabbed the elixir from its hiding place and drank the liquid herself. Its effects were instant and she immediately flew high into the sky until she reached the Moon, which she made her new home.

While she was sad to be parted from her husband, Chang'e knew she had done the right thing. And although she was forced to leave Yi behind, she had saved the world from evil.

Chang'e became immortal and flew to the heavens, where she became goddess of the Moon.

GODDESSES OF NATURE

Many people's lives are affected by the changing natural world, from stormy seas to explosive volcanoes. Goddesses, and their temper, are often thought to control these events.

Mari is a goddess of the Basque people from southwest Europe. She is in charge of many aspects of life, including the weather, and can cause fierce storms.

Sedna is the goddess of the sea and ruler of the Inuit underworld, known as Adlivun. She lives at the bottom of the sea.

A Chinese goddess of the sea, Mazu is worshipped in particular by sailors in the hope of good sailing conditions and plentiful fish.

MAHUIKA

PRONUNCIATION:
MA-hoo-ee-ka

CULTURE: Māori

Mahuika is a fire goddess of the Māori people from New Zealand. She gave the secret of fire to the hero Māui so that he could share it with humans.

KONOHANA

PRONUNCIATION:
KO-no-ha-na

CULTURE:
Japanese

Konohana is the Japanese goddess of volcanoes; in particular, Mount Fuji, which is the highest volcano in Japan. She is responsible for stopping eruptions.

PELE

PRONOUNCIATION:
PEH-lay

CULTURE:
Hawaiian

Pele is the Hawaiian goddess of fire and volcanoes. She is particularly important to the inhabitants of the island of Hawaii, which has two of the world's most active volcanoes on it.

OLOKUN

PRONUNCIATION:
o-LO-kun

CULTURE:
Yoruba

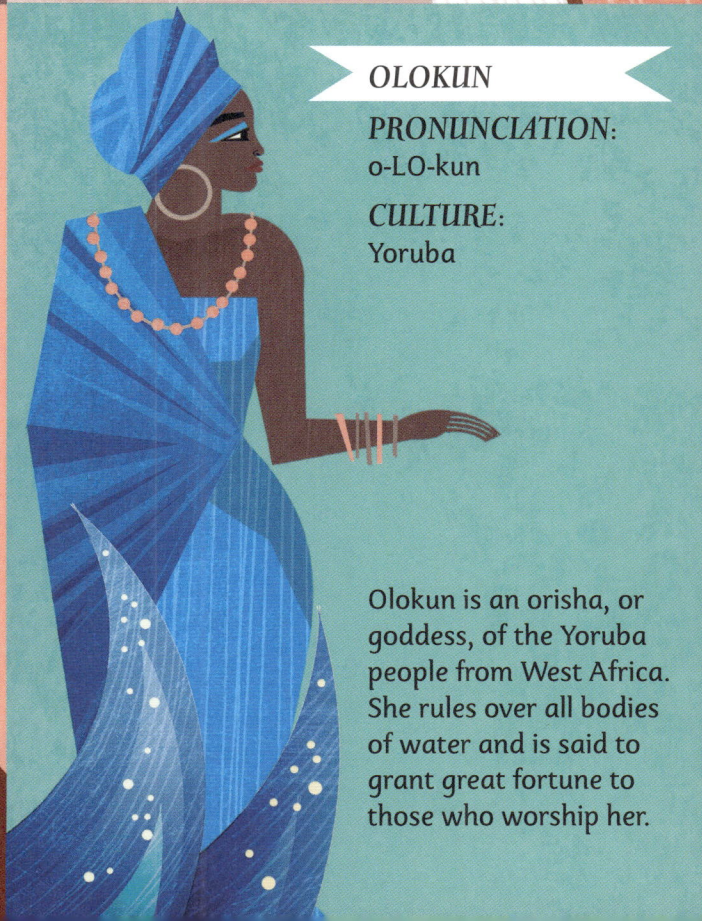

Olokun is an orisha, or goddess, of the Yoruba people from West Africa. She rules over all bodies of water and is said to grant great fortune to those who worship her.

33

Sedna's transformation

Sedna lived on a quiet shore with her father, where they made their living as fisherfolk. It had been only the two of them ever since she could remember.

Now that she was a young woman, however, men had begun to visit their home asking Sedna for her hand in marriage. Each time Sedna's answer was the same. "No, I will not marry you," she told them.

This went on for many months until the ice that covered the water began to crack and spring arrived. With the new season came the flock of fulmars, cousins of the albatross, who flew over Sedna's home annually. This year, however, was different.

The leader of the fulmars had been watching Sedna and this year he planned to ask her to be his wife.

Swooping down, he landed on the shore where the young woman stood watching the birds fly by. "Sedna, come to the land of the birds and marry me. My tent is made of the finest pelts and you will sleep on the softest seal skins," he said.

The fulmar's offer was more exciting than any Sedna had yet received, so she finally said yes. After saying goodbye to her father, she climbed onto her new husband's back and together they flew back across the water to the land of the birds.

When they arrived, however, Sedna's new home was not what she had expected. Instead of thick animal pelts, the tent was made of fish skins, which were full of holes that let in snow and rain. The soft seal furs she had been promised were nowhere to be seen. Instead, her bed was made of slippery whale blubber. Sedna was miserable.

A whole year passed in the land of the birds and each day Sedna cried for her old home, but her new husband refused to take her back. Fortunately, Sedna's father then decided to make the trip across the water to visit her.

When Sedna's father arrived, he was horrified by the life his daughter was leading.

Sedna's father demanded that her husband allow her to return home with him, but again the fulmar refused. Enraged, Sedna's father leapt at the bird and killed him, then swiftly carried his daughter onto his boat.

Together, father and daughter began the long journey home, but the other birds soon discovered what had happened to their leader. Furious, they flew after the tiny boat and with the combined power of their wings caused a mighty storm. The wind blew the boat from side to side and the waves crashed over the pair so that they spluttered and gasped.

Sedna's father began to panic. "This is all your fault," he yelled at his daughter, forgetting he had been the one who had killed the fulmar. "If I give you back, they will let me live."

Before Sedna could do anything to stop him, her father grabbed her by the waist and threw her over the side of the boat. However, she clung onto the side of the vessel with both hands. "Let go!" her father shouted, but she would not.

To Sedna's dismay, her father snatched his knife from his bag and brought it down on her fingers.

The severed fingertips fell into the sea and one by one they were transformed. The first five became graceful seals, while the second five turned into enormous whales. Meanwhile, no longer able to hold on, Sedna was swallowed by the sea.

As she sank, Sedna's body changed too. Below her waist she grew a fish's tale, and she found she was able to breathe underwater. She swam deep down to the bottom of the ocean and realized she was finally free from husbands and fathers alike, and there she remained, as goddess of the sea itself.

Konohana's labour

Konohana was the goddess of volcanoes, her favourite being Mount Fuji. She was strong and beautiful, but had a fiery temper.

One afternoon, Konohana was walking along the beach, enjoying the sea breeze and feeling the sand between her toes, when she met a young god. His name was Ninigi and he was the grandson of Amaterasu, goddess of the Sun.

Ninigi was immediately struck by Konohana's beauty and it was not long before he asked her for her hand in marriage. "I would marry you, but you will have to ask my father Ohoyamatsumi first," Konohana told him.

So, Ninigi went to Ohoyamatsumi and asked him for his daughter's hand. Ohoyamatsumi thought Ninigi a good match and told the man he might marry either of his daughters. Of course, Ninigi chose Konohana, and so the two were married.

The next day, Konohana had some news.

"I am expecting a child," she announced.
"Surely not!" exclaimed Ninigi. "We have been married only one night, the child cannot be mine."
Konohana was deeply hurt by her new husband's words. As she stood there, she felt a burning rage begin to grow inside her just like a volcano about to erupt. Waving her

hand, she conjured a doorless hut from thin air and transported herself inside. "If this baby is the great grandchild of the sun goddess, then they will be unharmed by fire. If not, they will surely perish," she called out.

In a moment, the hut went up in flames.

Inside the hut, Konohana went into labour and all alone she gave birth to not one but three baby boys. She named them Hoderi, Hoori, and Hosuseri, and each was unhurt by the flames around them. When Konohana emerged from the ashes of the hut, her loyalty was proven and Ninigi felt ashamed for doubting his wife.

The hut burned to the ground around Konohana.

39

Olokun's flood

For a time, Olokun, goddess of the sea, was the only god who lived on Earth. The other gods lived high in the heavens, including Obatala, god of the sky and creator of humankind.

Then, one day, countless gods began to descend from above and divide up the Earth's land between them. Infuriated, Olokun demanded to know what was going on.

"Obatala told us that we could each take a part of the Earth in order to rule over the humans who live on it," one of the gods explained.

"I was never consulted about this," Olokun grumbled. "How dare Obatala decide such things without me."

Olokun was determined to show Obatala what she thought of his idea. Filled with anger, she made the waters rise up from the sea. Waves crashed onto the

Olokun made the waters of the sea surge over the land.

land, flooding the homes and destroying the crops of the peoples who lived there. "That will show them," Olokun thought to herself.

When he learned what Olokun had done, Obatala was horrified, for he cared deeply for the people he had created. Olokun was a powerful goddess, however, and he did not want to make the problem worse. Obatala decided to seek the advice of Orunmila, the god of wisdom. "Do not fret, Obatala," said Orunmila. "I shall travel to the Earth and turn back the tides Olokun has unleashed."

And so, Orunmila descended to the world below and used his powers to calm the sea.

The waters quickly receded and the land became dry once again. Olokun was infuriated, but there was nothing she could do. If she sent another flood, Orunmila would surely just undo her actions again. It seemed, this time at least, she had been beaten and there was nothing she could do but sit and simmer in her anger.

Orunmila calmed the waves and pushed back the flood.

ERATO

PRONUNCIATION:
EH-ra-toh

CULTURE: Ancient Greek

Erato is one of the nine muses in ancient Greek and Roman mythology. The muses inspire mortals to create different forms of art. Erato is in charge of love poetry.

HI'IAKA

PRONUNCIATION:
HEE-ee-a-ka

CULTURE: Hawaiian

Hi'iaka is a Hawaiian goddess who was the first god to perform the ceremonial hula dance. Because of this, Hi'iaka is the goddess of hula and hula dancers.

BRIGID

PRONUNCIATION:
BRIH-jid

CULTURE: Irish

Brigid is one of the Tuatha Dé Danann, who are ancient gods from Ireland. She is goddess of a variety of things, including poetry, and is an expert dairywoman and brewer.

GODDESSES OF
ART, SINGING, AND DANCING

Whether it's poetry or dancing, weaving or storytelling, people have always looked to gods as supporters of their art. In particular, many hope to be granted with inspiration for new ideas.

ERZULIE FRÉDA

PRONOUNCIATION:
ER-zoo-lee FREH-da

CULTURE: Haitian

Erzulie Fréda is a goddess, or lwa, in the Vodou religion of Haiti. She is associated with many different things, including love, beauty, dancing, and jewellery.

BENZAITEN

PRONUNCIATION:
ben-ZAI-ten

CULTURE:
Japanese

SARASWATI

PRONUNCIATION:
SA-ra-swa-tee

CULTURE:
Hindu

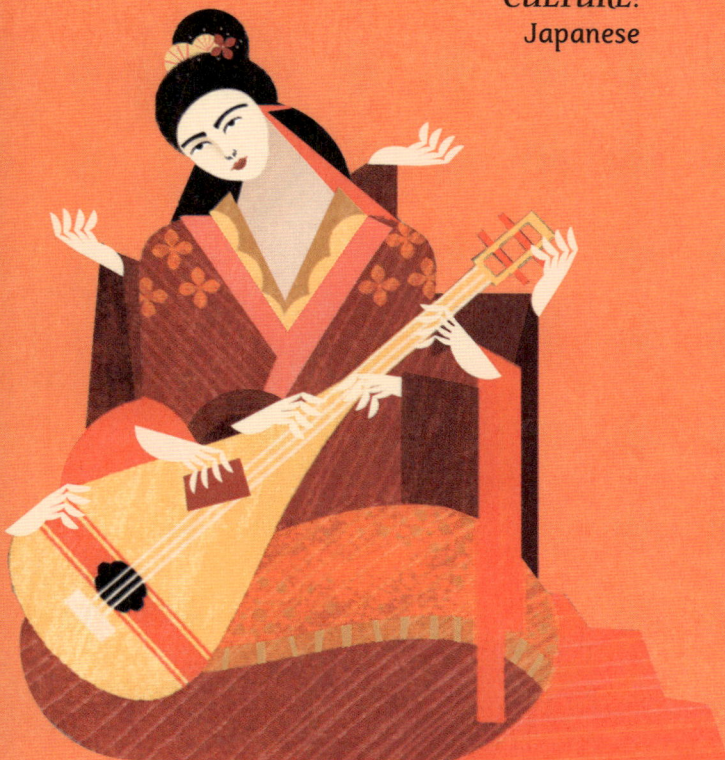

Benzaiten is a Japanese goddess of fortune, eloquence, and the arts. She is one of the seven lucky gods of Japan and can also turn into a dragon.

Saraswati is one of the three Hindu goddesses who make up the Tridevi, an important group of deities. She is the goddess of music and is often shown playing a veena.

43

Hi'iaka's quest

Hi'iaka, goddess of dancing, lived in a forest of vibrant red lehua trees on the island of Hawaii with her partner, a woman named Hopoe.

Hopoe was an expert in the ancient form of hula dancing and Hi'iaka loved her very much. The goddess spent her days fishing, singing, and learning the graceful movements of hula from Hopoe. All in all, they had a happy life.

One day, however, Hi'iaka heard the call of her older sister Pele, goddess of fire, from within the volcano Kilauea where she lived. Hi'iaka knew there would be trouble if she ignored her powerful older sister and so she left to travel deep inside the fiery mountain, leaving Hopoe to watch over their home. "Welcome sister," Pele greeted Hi'iaka. "I have a task for you. I have met the man I love in my dreams and his name is Lohi'au. As I cannot leave my mountain, I wish to have him join me here. So, it is up to you to fetch him for me, but you must return within forty days."

"Of course," Hiʻiaka replied. "But you must promise me that you will protect Hopoe and the forest in which we live while I am gone. Do not unleash your fire on the things dearest to me." For she knew how quickly Pele could become angry.

Pele agreed to the deal and Hiʻiaka began the long and difficult passage to the island of Kauaʻi where Lohiʻau lived.

Before Hiʻiaka left, Pele gave her a skirt of ferns made by the goddess of ferns herself, Pau-o-palae. This skirt wielded the power of lightning and would protect her on her way. In fact, when Pau-o-palae heard about Hiʻiaka's journey, she decided to join her, so the two set off together.

Hiʻiaka travelled to the volcano Kilauea where her sister Pele lived.

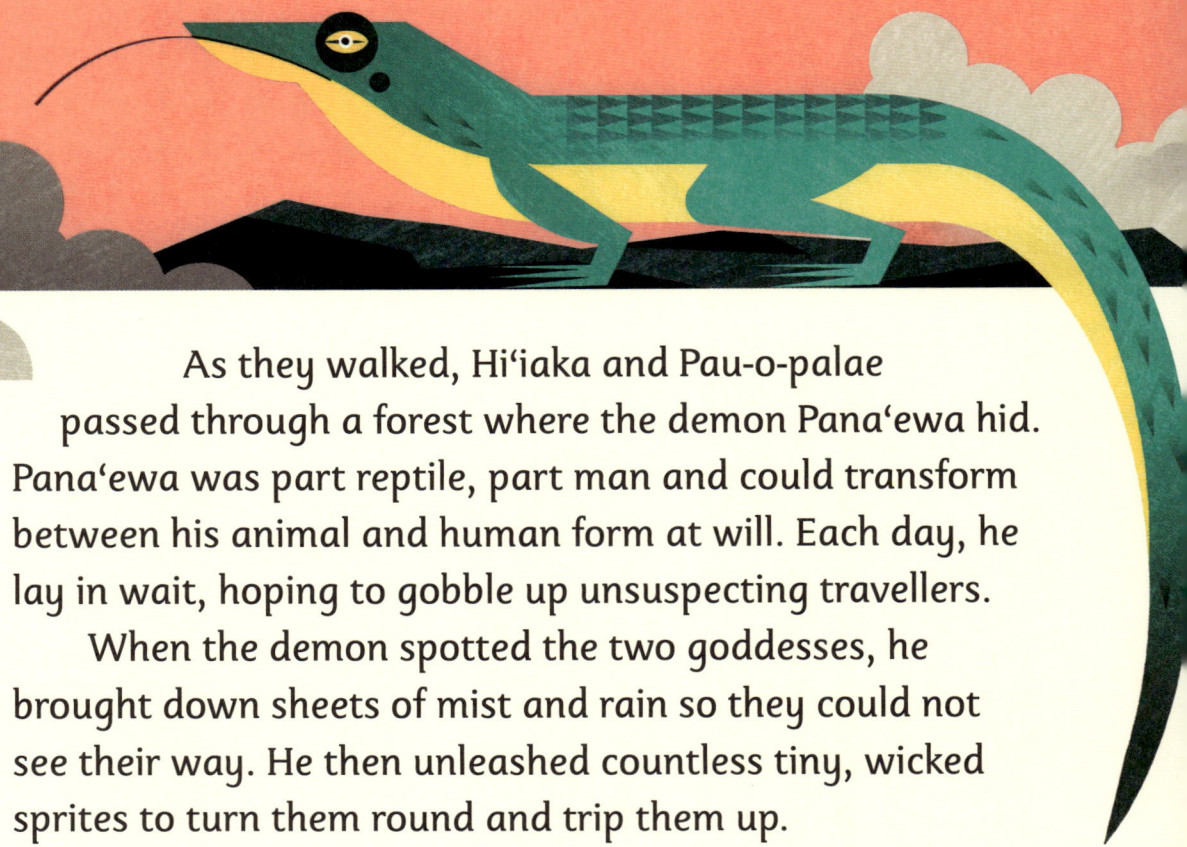

As they walked, Hiʻiaka and Pau-o-palae
passed through a forest where the demon Panaʻewa hid.
Panaʻewa was part reptile, part man and could transform
between his animal and human form at will. Each day, he
lay in wait, hoping to gobble up unsuspecting travellers.
When the demon spotted the two goddesses, he
brought down sheets of mist and rain so they could not
see their way. He then unleashed countless tiny, wicked
sprites to turn them round and trip them up.

Hiʻiaka, however, was prepared for such an event.

The goddess lifted her enchanted skirt and used the
ferns to sweep aside the mist so she could see the
way ahead. With another wave of the skirt,
she created bolts of lightning, which beat
back the rain and sprites. As the path
became clear, Hiʻiaka and Pau-o-palae
began to run and, breathless but alive, they
escaped the forest.
This was not the only danger Hiʻiaka and
Pau-o-palae faced while travelling to Kauaʻi,

however, and because of this the journey was much slower than they had hoped. In fact, the forty days that Pele had given her sister had passed already when the younger goddess finally arrived at the home of Lohi'au.

With no sign of Hi'iaka, Pele began to fear her sister had run away with the man she loved.

Pele raged and stormed, and fiery lava flowed down from her volcanic home.

Molten rock spewed from Kilauea, destroying everything it touched, including Hi'iaka's forest home. Eventually, Pele's fury found Hopoe, who had run in terror to the nearby shore. The lava surrounded her, encasing her so that when the goddess finally stopped her rampage, Hopoe had been transformed into a gigantic boulder.

Despite Pele's doubts, Hi'iaka did finally return with Lohi'au. When she discovered what had happened to her home and to Hopoe, Hi'iaka was overwhelmed with sorrow. She sat faithfully beside the boulder, and as she watched, saw it rocking in the wind as if dancing still.

Benzaiten's blessing

The goddess of many different things, Benzaiten had eight arms and was very powerful. She was even able to transform into a dragon in a flash.

Among other people, Benzaiten looked after both artists and warriors. Many of them came from far and wide to visit her shrine and pray. Benzaiten's shrine was famous throughout the land because it was built upon an island of glittering crystal that jutted up from the centre of a wide lake, called Lake Biwa.

One day, a man who Benzaiten had never seen before arrived at the shrine. His name was Tsunemasa.

Tsunemasa was a warrior and he often fought in great battles.

Tsunemasa hoped to gain the goddess's favour, so that she would grant him luck when fighting. "Divine goddess, protector of warriors, you give me hope for the future," Tsunemasa declared upon entering the shrine.

The warrior's words pleased Benzaiten. She continued to watch with excitement as the monks who served her brought the

Benzaiten appeared as a splendid white dragon.

stranger a biwa, a stringed instrument like a lute, for Benzaiten loved music above all else. Tsunemasa picked up the biwa and began to play Benzaiten's secret songs. His skill with the biwa was unparalleled, and as his fingers danced over the strings, Benzaiten could not help but sway to the music.

Finally, moved by his playing, Benzaiten appeared in the form of a beautiful white dragon.

At the sight of the goddess, Tsunemasa began to cry. "Does this mean you have accepted my prayers?" he sobbed, overwhelmed with joy. In answer, Benzaiten only nodded her head, but Tsunemasa knew that he had the blessing of the goddess. From that day, he was sure that all his enemies would be defeated and his people kept safe.

Tsunemasa began to play the biwa for Benzaiten.

49

GODDESSES OF ANIMALS

Humans have always lived alongside animals. Some provide food and some are admired, while others are too dangerous to approach, but in many cultures, they too are watched over by goddesses.

WHITE BUFFALO CALF WOMAN

PRONUNCIATION:
-

CULTURE: Indigenous People of North America

White Buffalo Calf Woman is a goddess from North America who is particularly important to the Lakota people. She taught them sacred rituals and restored buffalo to the land.

MEDEINA

PRONUNCIATION:
meh-DEE-na

CULTURE:
Lithuanian

Medeina is a Lithuanian goddess of trees and animals. She is also a huntress who has never married and lives in the forest with her pack of wolves.

DALI

PRONUNCIATION:
DAH-lee

CULTURE:
Georgian

The Georgian goddess of hunting and mountain animals, Dali watches over deer and wild goats. She uses her long, golden hair to tie up hunters that are greedy and then dangles them over chasms.

NGANU LEIMA

PRONUNCIATION:
n-GA-noo LAY-ma

CULTURE:
Meitei

Nganu Leima is the Meitei goddess of ducks and other waterbirds. She shares a human husband with her two sisters. The Meitei people are from northeast India.

EPONA

PRONUNCIATION:
eh-POH-na

CULTURE: Celtic

Epona is the Celtic goddess of horses, donkeys, and ponies. She was worshipped in both Britain and Gaul — an ancient area of France — and in ancient Rome. The Romans even held a festival in her honour in December.

White Buffalo Calf Woman's lessons

One day, two young men were out hunting for game. As they climbed a hill, they stopped in their tracks when an unfamiliar figure appeared in front of them.

The men watched in awe as a beautiful young woman dressed in buckskin clothing floated towards them, her feet never touching the ground. The first man was the more arrogant of the two and, without asking permission, stretched out his hand to touch the woman.

In that moment, white lightning flashed across the sky.

Before the second man knew what had happened, there remained only ashes where his companion had once stood. "Return to your home and tell your chief to prepare for my visit," the woman told the second man.

The young hunter nodded and rushed back to share what had happened with his people and their chief, Standing Hollow Horn.

When everyone heard the news, they immediately began to get ready for the woman's arrival.

After four days and four nights, the woman approached, carrying a bundle in her hands. Standing Hollow Horn greeted her with great respect and invited her to join him inside. Pleased with his behaviour, the woman drew from her bundle a chanunpa, or ceremonial pipe. "I have come to teach you seven ceremonies through which you will honour the cycle of nature," she said.

Everyone listened closely as the woman taught them how to use the pipe and practise each of the seven ceremonies.

When the woman was satisfied that they had learned everything she had to show them, she set off on her way again. Before she was out of sight, however, the woman stopped and rolled along the ground. With each roll she transformed: first into a black buffalo, then a brown buffalo, and next a red buffalo. With a final spin, she became a magnificent white buffalo.

From then on, the hunter and his people received everything they needed from the buffalo, from meat to eat to hide for clothing. But they never took more than they needed, remembering their part in the cycle of nature.

The woman rolled on the ground and became a white buffalo.

Dali's disguise

Dali was a goddess who lived in the mountains. She watched over the hoofed animals that shared her home, including wild goats and deer.

The goddess was also pregnant, and one day Dali woke to find she had begun to go into labour. Alone, she settled herself on the edge of the mountain and gave birth to a tiny, wailing baby.

Dali was exhausted from her efforts, however, and the child slipped from her hands and tumbled down the side of the cliff. To add to her horror, a gigantic wolf sat waiting at the bottom of the mountain, where it caught the baby in its jaws.

Luckily, a hunter named Mepisa had witnessed the whole event. Without hesitation, he jumped into action and, raising his rifle, fired at the animal.

The loud bang startled the wolf, which dropped the baby, and Mepisa caught the boy in his arms.

"You have saved my child," cried the goddess Dali. "Allow me to repay your kindness with one of three gifts. Every day you may receive a small mountain goat, or else each September you will be gifted nine large turs. Or, finally, you may come and live with me."

Now, turs were a goat only found in the Caucasus Mountains and were highly sought-after, and Mepisa leapt at the chance to receive so many. "Thank you goddess," Mepisa replied. "I will accept your offer of nine turs every year."

When September arrived, Dali sent the herd of turs to Mepisa just as she had promised. Curious to see the hunter again, she decided to disguise herself as a goat with golden horns and follow along. Mepisa, however, who did not realize what the golden gleam of the horns must mean, naively shot at Dali herself.

The bullet whizzed through the air and ricocheted off Dali's horns straight back at Mepisa, mortally wounding him. And so Mepisa's life came to a tragic end, leaving only Dali and her child with the memory of his bravery.

The bullet bounced off Dali's horns, back at Mepisa.

For as long as people have worshipped gods, they have prayed to them for help in love and war. While these two things seem very different, they sometimes share the same goddess.

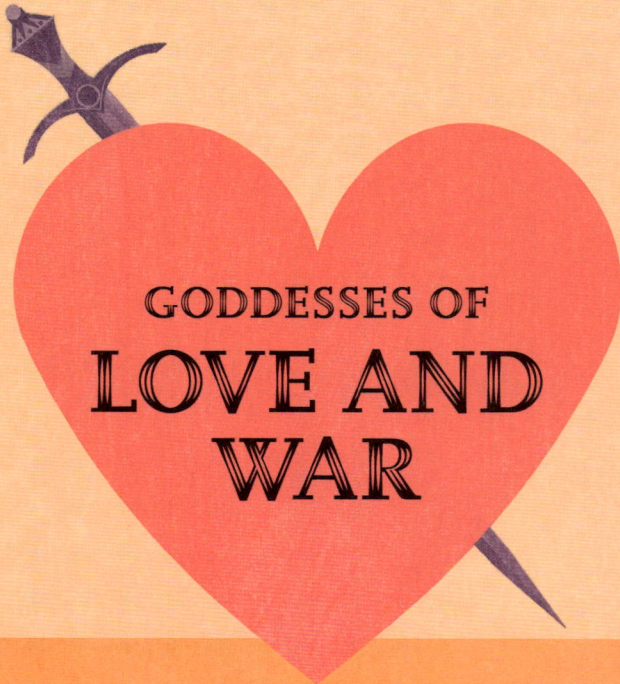

GODDESSES OF LOVE AND WAR

THE MORRIGÁN

PRONUNCIATION: mor-i-GAHN

CULTURE: Irish

The Morrigán is a goddess in Irish legend who often appears on battlefields as a sign of doom to warriors. She is sometimes shown as one woman, and at other times as three separate women. She can also transform into a raven.

INANNA

PRONUNCIATION: ih-NAH-na

CULTURE: Akkadian and Sumerian

Inanna is both a goddess of love and war, and the queen of heaven in Sumerian religion. She was also worshipped by the Akkadians as Ishtar. The Sumerian and Akkadian empires were both found in ancient Mesopotamia.

FREYA

PRONUNCIATION: FREY-yah

CULTURE: Norse

Freya is the goddess of both love and death in Norse mythology. She receives half of the warriors who die bravely in battle in the afterlife. Her chariot is drawn by two cats and she has a feathered cloak that lets her fly.

ANAT

PRONUNCIATION: A-nat

CULTURE: Amorite and ancient Egyptian

HATHOR

PRONUNCIATION: HA-thor

CULTURE: Ancient Egyptian

Hathor is the ancient Egyptian cow-headed goddess of love. However, she can transform into another goddess, Sekhmet. In this form, she has a lioness's head and is the goddess of war.

Anat is a goddess of war and hunting who was first worshipped by the Amorite people from ancient Syria more than 4,000 years ago. She also became popular in ancient Egypt during the reign of Ramesses II.

Inanna's rescue

Inanna was a powerful goddess who ruled over both love and war. However, she was deeply annoyed that despite her power, she was not able to visit the underworld.

No one except the messengers of her sister Ereshkigal, goddess of the underworld, were allowed to enter its dark depths and leave again. This didn't deter Inanna though, who decided that regardless of the rules, she would make the trip there.

Inanna approached the first gate to the underworld and demanded entry. "If you do not let me in, I will smash down the door itself," she cried. So, the gatekeeper opened the gate, but first he explained that Inanna must remove her crown.

One by one, Inanna passed through the seven gates to the underworld and at each, she was forced to discard one of her items of jewellery until she arrived at the court of Ereshkigal.

Ereshkigal was furious to see Inanna. "You will never leave this realm my sister," Ereshkigal stated, before placing Inanna into a deep sleep.

With Inanna trapped in the underworld, love faded from the Earth.

Enki, god of wisdom, was very distressed by this development. Without Inanna, animals ceased having young and mortals stopped having babies. So, he came up with a plan. First, he created a beautiful person named Asu-shu-namir, whom he commanded to rescue Inanna. "Go to the underworld Asu-shu-namir and say the names of the great gods," Enki said. "Once you have done so, Ereshkigal will give you whatever you ask for, including the waters of life."

Asu-shu-namir travelled to the underworld just as instructed, and recited the names of the great gods. Ereshkigal was frustrated, but there was nothing she could do. When Asu-shu-namir asked for the waters of life, she had to hand them over.

Then, Asu-shu-namir sprinkled the waters over Inanna's motionless body, waking her from her slumber. Together, the two passed back through the seven gates and returned to the land of the living, restoring love to its inhabitants once more.

Ereshkigal was angry that Inanna had entered the underworld.

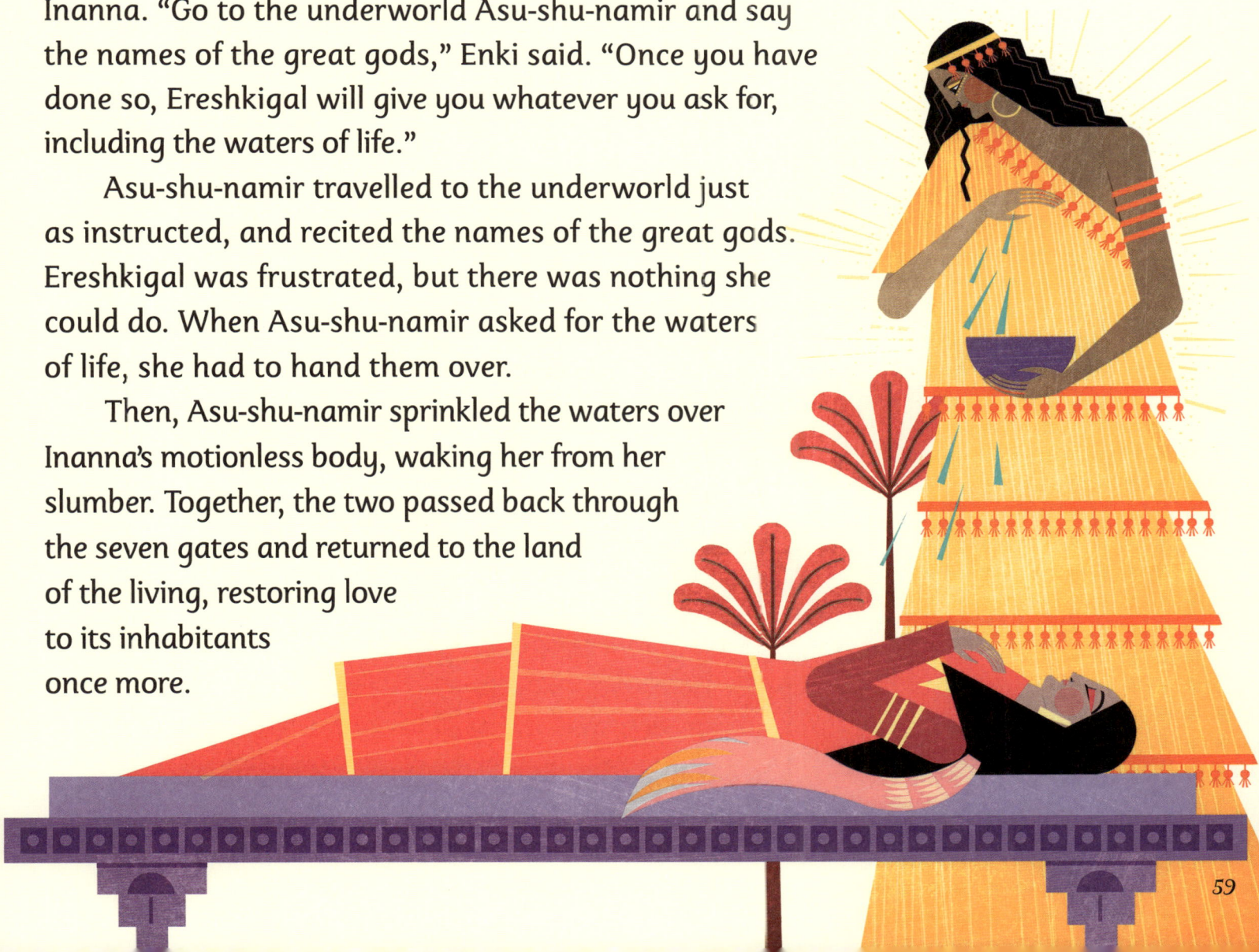

59

Hathor's alter ego

Ra, the king of the gods, was under threat from a group of humans who wished to overthrow him. He thought for many hours about how to defeat them.

It was Ra's eye that provided the solution. Ra plucked an eye from his face and, using his powers, transformed it into a goddess with the head of a cow. This was Hathor, goddess of love. "It is your job to punish the humans who have betrayed me," Ra told Hathor. "Seek out and destroy them." And off she went to kill the rebellious mortals.

Hathor tracked down the humans one by one and slayed them, but all this violence changed the goddess. Whenever she killed someone, she transformed into another goddess entirely: Sekhmet, the lion-headed goddess of war.

As Sekhmet, Hathor found she liked the taste of blood and even after her task was complete, she decided to carry on her rampage.

The goddess marched across the deserts of Egypt striking down every human she met. Ra grew concerned that Hathor had lost her way and would

not stop until every last human was gone. So, he set about devising a plan to stop her. First, he had a priest mix together the finest beer with the dust of crushed red ochre, a rock used for dyeing. The resulting liquid, he was pleased to see, looked exactly like blood.

Next, Ra sent his followers to pour seven thousand jars of the red beer across a field that lay in Sekhmet's path. When Sekhmet reached the field and saw what she thought was blood, she assumed that this must have been the site of a recent battle.

Happily, she began to drink the blood, but was surprised by its taste.

"What is this liquid?" Sekhmet asked aloud. "It's like no blood I've tasted before." On hearing her words, Ra, who had been waiting nearby, revealed himself. "This is a drink that can only be prepared by humans," he explained. "However, if you kill them all, they will no longer be able to make it."

"Then I shall strike them down no more, for this is better than any blood," she replied. Before Ra's eyes Sekhmet transformed into Hathor once more, and finally her rampage was over for good.

Anat's friend

Anat was the goddess of war and a good friend of the weather god Baal. One day, she received a visit from Baal's messenger.

The messenger had come to invite Anat to celebrate with Baal, for he had recently won a battle against the sea god Yam. Anat agreed and when she arrived, she was greeted warmly by her friend. They talked a while over dinner, but Anat could not help but notice that Baal's mood seemed to dampen as the hours passed. "Tell me, friend, what makes you so sad when you have had such success?" she asked.

Baal sighed. "I wish to have a palace of my own, one that suits my station like the other gods," he explained. "For I have no permanent home."

It seemed a reasonable enough request but El, the ruler of the gods, did not like Baal.

Anat wanted to aid her friend. "If it would help, I will go to El on your behalf and ask that he have a

palace built for you," she offered. Baal's face lit up at this suggestion and he gratefully agreed.

So, Anat went to El, but the god was not inclined to hear her request and sent her away again. Anat, however, had a back-up plan! She gathered some gifts and took them to Asherah, the mother goddess, and El's wife. "Please will you convince El to build Baal a home?" asked Anat. "A god like him deserves a palace."

Luckily, Asherah liked Anat, and she liked presents even more.

So, the mother goddess agreed to Anat's request and went to talk to her husband. El did not like to say no to Asherah and finally he gave in. He summoned his divine craftsmen and gave them instructions to build a new palace befitting a god. And that was how Anat helped Baal get his home.

Baal was overjoyed to finally have his own palace.

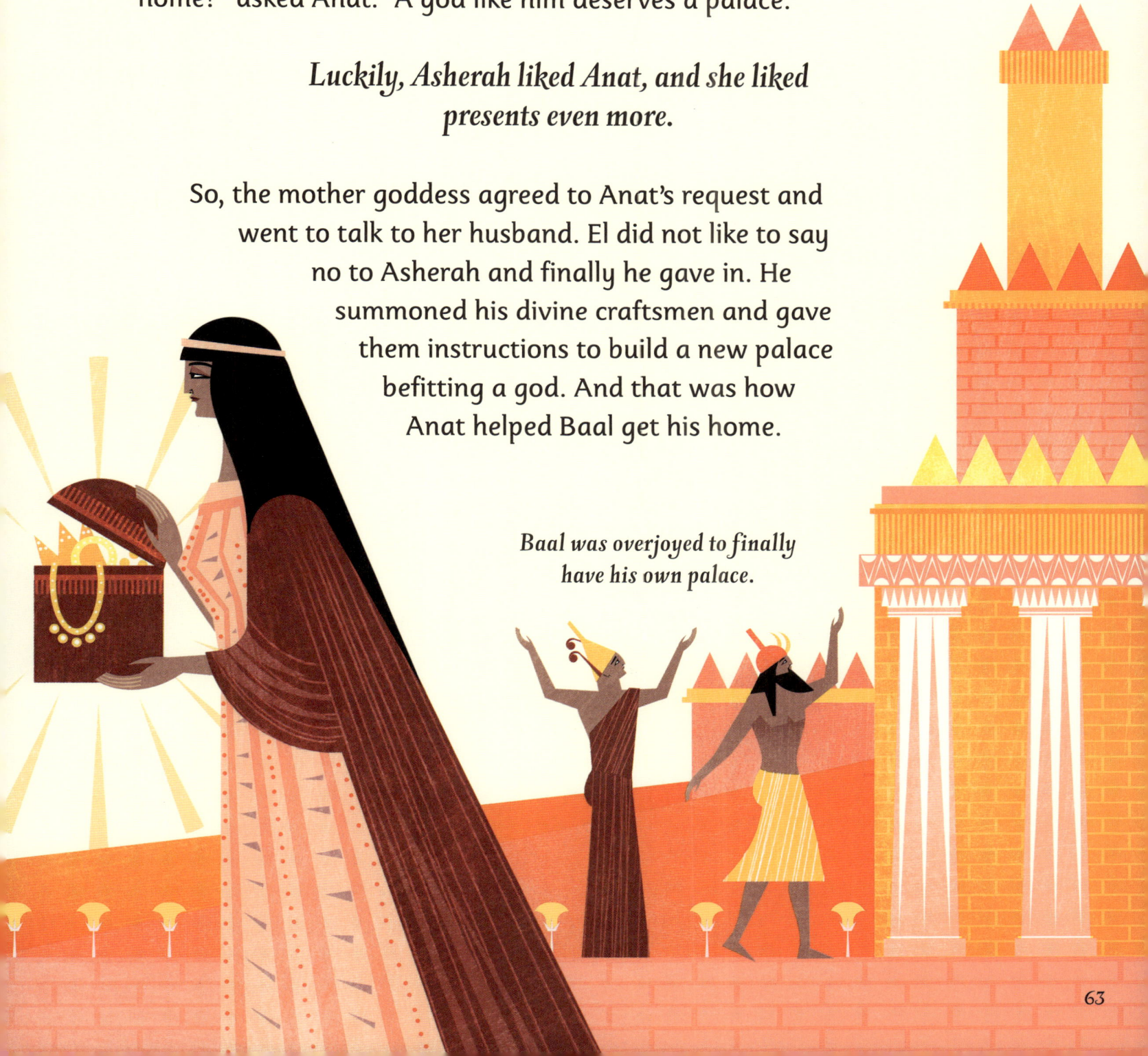

UNIQUE GODDESSES

Some goddesses cannot be easily categorized. They often watch over very specific areas that are not always represented by gods in other cultures. From fertilizer to door hinges, they protect the smallest aspects of life.

AXOMAMMA

PRONUNCIATION: AKS-oh-ma-ma

CULTURE: Inca

Axomamma is the Inca goddess of potatoes and a daughter of the mother goddess Pachamama. The Inca people lived in Peru, where the potato is from.

CARDEA

PRONUNCIATION: KAR-dee-a

CULTURE: Ancient Roman

Cardea is the ancient Roman goddess of door hinges. She has the important role of allowing entry to homes and other dwellings.

TLAZOLTEOTL

PRONUNCIATION: tla-zol-tay-OH-tel
CULTURE: Aztec

Tlazolteotl is an Aztec goddess who rules over many things, including fertilizer. She eats dirt and makes plants grow. As well as this, she looks after women during childbirth.

ZIGU

PRONUNCIATION: ZI-goo
CULTURE: Chinese

One of the six household gods from ancient China, Zigu is specifically responsible for toilets. She was originally a woman who was sadly murdered, and then became a goddess.

LES LAVANDIÈRES

PRONUNCIATION: LEH la-von-dee-AIR
CULTURE: Celtic

Les Lavandières are a group of three goddesses from Celtic mythology shown as elderly washerwomen. They wash the clothing of those who are about to die, even foretelling people's deaths.

Zigu's return

Once, a man named Zixu was in love with a young woman named Zigu, who lived and worked in his home.

However, Zixu was already married to a woman named Cao, who hated Zigu. For this reason, Cao always gave Zigu the filthiest chores around the house, from clearing out the pigsty to scrubbing down the toilets.

Just doling out nasty tasks to Zigu was not enough for Cao, though. She grew more and more angry and jealous, until one day she snapped. Cao snuck up on Zigu while she was cleaning the toilet and struck the young woman, killing her where she stood.

Unknown to Cao, a messenger to the gods had witnessed Zigu's death.

The messenger took pity on the poor young woman who had done nothing but serve her household. "I will make you a goddess," the messenger told

Zigu's ghost. "You will never be forgotten, and mortals will honour your memory each year on this day as you were never honoured in life."

And so they did. From then on, when the fifteenth day of the first month arrived, people across the land stood by their toilets or their pigsties and invited the spirit of Zigu into their homes.

Wine and fruits were set out for the spirit of the young woman.

When Zigu arrived, she danced and sang to entertain her hosts. Finally, each person would ask Zigu what they should expect from the year to come, and the goddess would make predictions for their future. Just as the messenger had promised, Zigu was celebrated as a goddess as she had never been as a mortal.

Zigu's spirit was invited to return on the anniversary of her death each year.

MAGICAL BEINGS

Fairies, mermaids, witches, and shapeshifters – there are many magical beings who take the form of women. They live on Earth and often interact with people, but whether they use their abilities for good or for evil, all depends on each individual.

The beings you are about to meet have powers that no person could hope to possess. A few clever mortals, however, are able to outsmart them.

BLODEUWEDD

PRONUNCIATION: blod-AI-weth

CULTURE: Welsh

In Welsh legend, Blodeuwedd is created by magicians out of meadowsweet and broom flowers. She married the hero Lleu Llaw, who was cursed never to marry a human woman. She betrayed him, however, and was transformed into an owl as punishment.

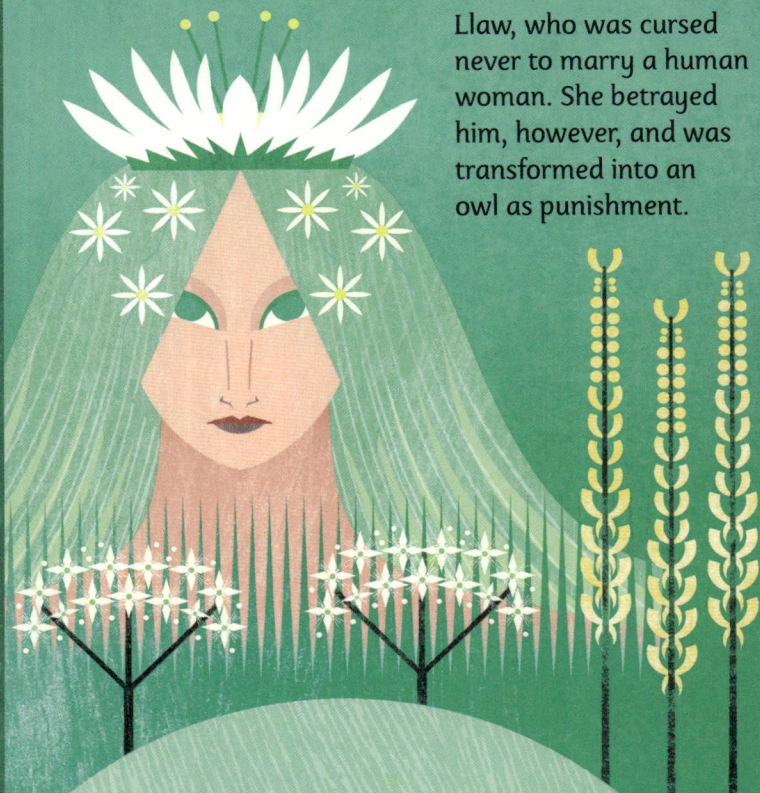

CIGUAPA

PRONUNCIATION: sih-GWA-pa

CULTURE: Dominican

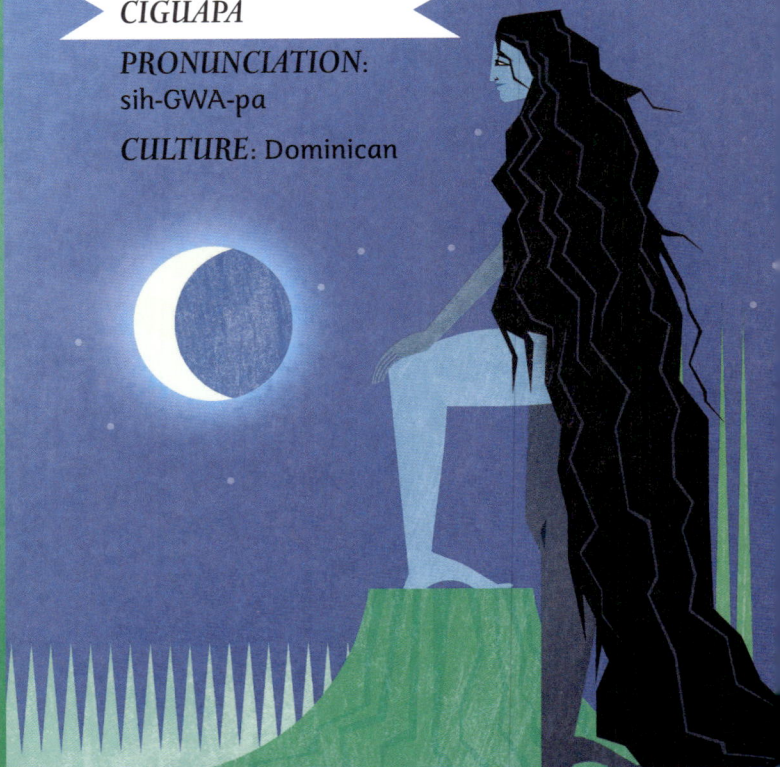

Ciguapas are mythical creatures from the mountains and forests of the Dominican Republic. They resemble women, and are known for their beauty as well as their blue skin and backward-facing feet.

FAIRIES AND NATURE SPIRITS

WHUPPITY STOORIE

PRONUNCIATION: WUP-it-ee STOO-ree

CULTURE: Scottish

Whuppity Stoorie is an evil fairy in Scottish folklore. She tries to steal babies by striking devious deals with their mothers when they are in need.

The world is full of marvels, from tree-packed forests to snow-capped mountains. It is not surprising then that legends are full of beings who live in and care for these magical places.

RHIANNON

PRONUNCIATION: rhee-A-non

CULTURE: Welsh

Queen of the fairies in Welsh mythology, Rhiannon is incredibly clever. She is closely associated with horses and is known for her refusal to marry a man until she fell in love.

ÂU CƠ

PRONUNCIATION: OH KHER

CULTURE: Vietnamese

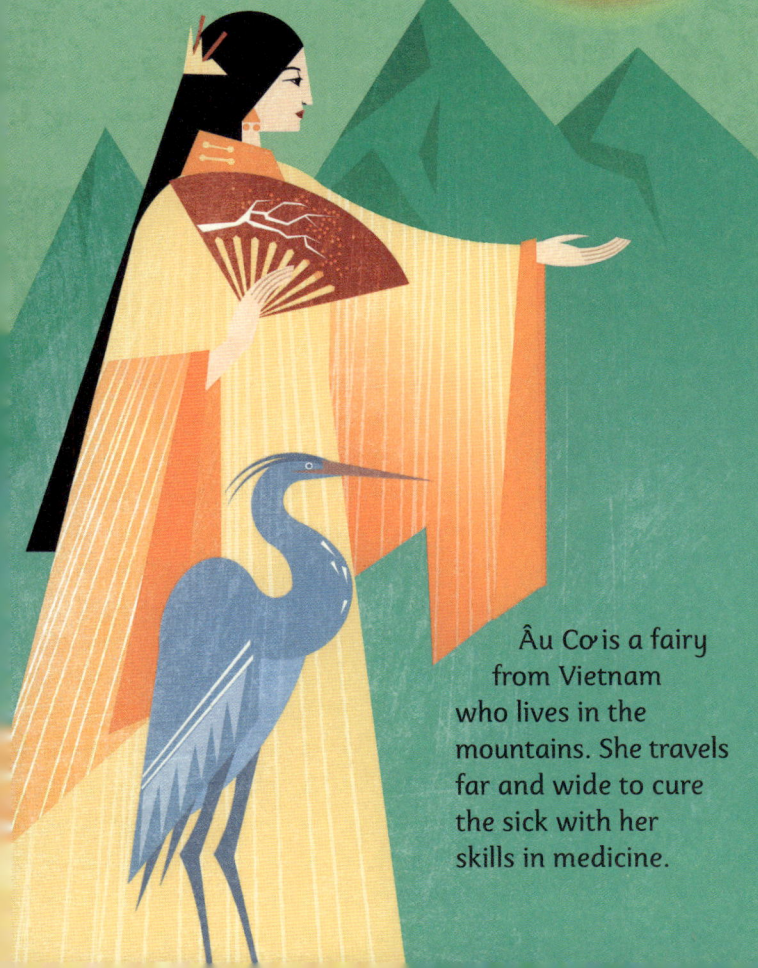

Âu Cơ is a fairy from Vietnam who lives in the mountains. She travels far and wide to cure the sick with her skills in medicine.

LA MADREMONTE

PRONUNCIATION: LA ma-dreh-MON-tay

CULTURE: Colombian

La Madremonte is a vengeful spirit from Colombia. She protects the forest and the animals in it, punishing those who harm them.

Rhiannon's wedding

The fairy Rhiannon had long been betrothed to a man named Gwawl. Rhiannon, however, had no feelings for Gwawl at all. Instead, she wished only to marry Pwyll, the Prince of Dyfed.

Rhiannon had been watching Pwyll for many months, while staying invisible. However, one day, she decided to reveal herself. Pwyll was sat upon a magical mound that he had been told would show those worthy enough something marvellous. As he watched, Rhiannon appeared, dressed in exquisite golden robes and seated upon an enormous white horse. He knew immediately that this was the woman he was meant to marry.

Jumping onto his own horse, the prince attempted to catch up, but no matter how fast he rode, Rhiannon was always the same distance in front. "Please wait for me!" Pwyll called out.

On hearing his words, Rhiannon pulled her horse to a stop.

"Of course. Although I think your horse would have appreciated it if you had asked me a little sooner," she said laughing, and nodded at his exhausted steed.

"Tell me why you visit this realm?" Pwyll asked.

"My father would have me marry a man against my will, but I would rather you were my husband, brave prince," Rhiannon replied.

Pwyll was overjoyed. "Why, of course I will marry you!" he cried.

So, the two set a date, and exactly one year from that day they sat down to feast before they were joined in marriage. Soon their celebrations were disturbed, however, by an uninvited guest. "I have come to ask a favour," the stranger said to Pwyll.

"Make your request and if it is within my power, you will have it," Pwyll answered.

At his words, Rhiannon groaned. "Why would you make such a promise without first knowing what this man seeks? You have made a foolish mistake," she said.

"Why, who is this man?" Pwyll exclaimed.

"My name is Gwawl," responded the stranger. "And I wish for Rhiannon's hand in marriage."

Now, Pwyll had made a promise in front of his court, and he was bound by his word. Fortunately, Rhiannon had an idea. "Take this," she said offering Pwyll a small sack. "When the day comes for my marriage to Gwawl, make your own request to him. Ask to fill your sack with food. The bag is magic and can never be filled. As he grows impatient, tell him your bag will carry all the food in the world unless a nobleman stands inside and squashes the contents down. When he does this, you must flip the sack upside down and tie it shut, trapping him inside."

When the day came for Gwawl and Rhiannon to be wed, Pwyll arrived as instructed with the magical sack. "Please allow me to fill my bag with some food from your feast," Pwyll asked Gwawl. It seemed such a small thing that Gwawl agreed immediately. As he watched though, he was appalled to see Pwyll continue to take more and more food from their table. "When will your bag be full?" Gwawl demanded.

Pwyll explained to Gwawl what Rhiannon had told him and Gwawl immediately volunteered for the job.

Just as Gwawl set his feet atop the food, however, Pwyll twirled the sack into the air and tied the knot on top as tightly as he could. "Let me out!" yelled Gwawl from inside. "Only if you'll let Pwyll and me be wed instead," Rhiannon replied.

"Fine!" Gwawl screamed, recognizing he was beaten. And so, that very same night, Rhiannon and Prince Pwyll sat down at their wedding feast, and this time nothing could stop their marriage.

Pwyll swung the bag over his head, trapping Gwawl inside.

Whuppity Stoorie's puzzle

Whuppity Stoorie was a difficult fairy to deal with. Unfortunately for one young woman, the fairy called upon her when she was in trouble.

The young woman's husband had run off, leaving her and her baby with nothing but a prized pig. That morning, however, the pig had fallen ill. "The pig is all I have," the woman wailed.

"Allow me to help," came a croaky voice. When the woman turned round, she saw an older woman standing in the doorway of the barn.

"If you can help me, I will give you whatever you ask!" the young woman pleaded. What she didn't know was that she was speaking to a fairy.

So, the fairy knelt by the pig and whispered a few magic words.

With a great snort, the pig heaved itself onto its hooves and began to shuffle around the barn as good as new. "Now that I have saved your pig I will take your baby," the fairy said, pointing to the bundle in the woman's arms.

"Not my son!" cried the woman.

"You promised me whatever I want. But as the laws of my people require, I will give you three days before you must give him to me. If in that time you can guess my name, then you shall keep the child." And with those words, the fairy was gone.

The young woman barely slept that night, so in the morning she decided to go for a walk in the nearby forest. As she wandered, she heard someone singing a little way ahead, and what she heard astounded her.

"The woman will never guess my name, for I am Whuppity Stoorie," sang the voice.

It was the fairy! The woman ran back home as quick as a hare and waited two more days for the fairy to arrive. "Time to give me your child," came the fairy's call as she approached.

"I don't think so WHUPPITY STOORIE," cried the woman. At the sound of her name, the fairy screamed and away she fled, leaving the young woman and her son to live in peace once more.

Whuppity Stoorie healed the woman's pig and demanded her son in return.

77

PINCOYA

PRONUNCIATION:
pin-KOI-ya

CULTURE: Chilean

Pincoya is a mermaid who lives in the seas surrounding the island of Chiloé near Chile. She provides the local people with fish.

MERMAIDS AND WATER SPIRITS

The Earth is covered by bodies of water, from oceans to streams. Many creatures are believed to live within their depths, including water spirits and fish-tailed mermaids.

IARA

PRONUNCIATION:
ee-AH-ra

CULTURE: Brazilian

Iara is a Brazilian mermaid with long, green hair. She lures men into drowning by singing because she was betrayed by the men in her own family.

MELUSINE

PRONUNCIATION:
MEL-yoo-seen

CULTURE: French

In French legend, Melusine is a water spirit and daughter of a fairy named Pressina. Her mother cursed her to have a serpent's tail one day out of each week.

PANIA

PRONUNCIATION:
PAH-nee-a

CULTURE: Māori

In New Zealand, Pania is a mermaid who lives off the coast of North Island. She married a Māori man, but eventually returned to her people under the water.

LIRIOPE

PRONUNCIATION:
lee-ree-OHP-ee
CULTURE:
Ancient Greek

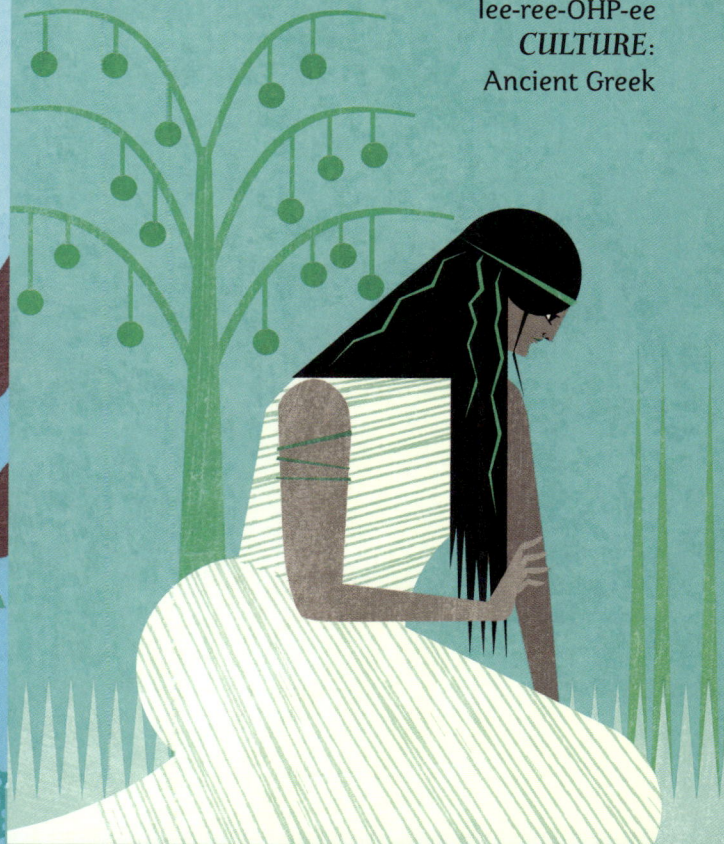

Liriope is a water spirit called a naiad from ancient Greek mythology. Naiads live in, and take care of, rivers, lakes, and streams. She was the mother of the beautiful youth Narcissus.

MAMAN DLO

PRONUNCIATION:
MA-mon DLOH

CULTURE: Trinidadian and Tobagonian

Maman Dlo, which means "mother of the river", is a water spirit from the Caribbean. From the waist down, she has an enormous serpent's tail instead of legs.

79

Pania's betrayal

In the ocean by New Zealand's North Island,
there lived a mermaid named Pania. Every night,
she swam along the shore and watched the
stars twinkling in the sky.

One evening, Pania had risen from the water to relax, hidden by
some large bushes of long-leaved flax, when she was spied by a
man. He was the local chief and he was very handsome. Pania
found herself captivated by his smile.

That night, Pania returned with the chief to his
home where they were married.

While Pania and the chief loved each other deeply, every
morning when the Sun rose, Pania would return to the seafolk
under the waves, and only came home when night fell once more.
Some months later, Pania gave birth to a son, and she called
him Moremore. At first, the chief was overjoyed, but soon he

The chief
placed cooked
food on Pania
and Moremore
as they slept.

grew worried that he might lose his son to the seafolk. He decided
to ask an elder of his people how he might stop this from happening.
"Simply place cooked food on your wife and child while they sleep,
and they will never leave again," the elder said.

The chief did as he was instructed, but he made one mistake.

The food he had placed on Pania and Moremore was not cooked all the
way through, so it had no effect. The next morning when Pania woke, she
realized that her husband had betrayed her trust, and with sadness in
her heart knew it was time to leave. She and Moremore left their
home that night and the chief never saw them again.

Melusine's curse

Melusine was the daughter of a fairy named Pressina. When she was fifteen years old, Melusine offended Pressina, who put a curse upon her daughter that she could tell no one about.

Some years later, Melusine was paddling in the Fountain of Thirst, enjoying the sunny day, when a young man approached on horseback. "Good day, Mademoiselle. My name is Raymond, Count of Poitou, may I ask for yours?"

Melusine thought the count was very handsome and she happily shared her name with him.

The young couple spent the whole day talking and found they had much in common. Soon Raymond asked Melusine for her hand in marriage. "I would love nothing more than to marry you, Raymond," she said. "However, you must promise me one thing."

"Anything!" he declared.

"You must never visit me on Saturdays, no matter what, and you cannot ask me why," Melusine replied.

It seemed such a small thing at the time that Raymond eagerly agreed and the two were soon wed. For a while Raymond kept his promise, but as the years went by, he grew more and more curious about his wife's request.

Finally, he gave in to his curiosity and he decided to spy on Melusine.

Raymond snuck up to his wife's room and opened the door just a crack. What he saw shocked him. While she was still his wife from the waist up, Melusine's legs had been replaced by a huge serpent's tail, and from her back sprouted leathery wings. He jumped out to confront her. "You are a serpent!" he yelled, frightening Melusine with his fury.

"Yes, now you know my secret, and now I know how untrustworthy my husband has turned out to be," Melusine cried. "For that reason, I must leave. You will never see my face again." And she fled from her husband never to return.

Maman Dlo's enchantment

The rivers of Trinidad and Tobago were watched over by a powerful spirit named Maman Dlo. She protected the waters and the animals in them.

The upper half of Maman Dlo's body was that of an old woman with long hair and tattoos covering her skin. The lower half, however, was that of an enormous serpent. She lived underwater, guarding her realm against any unwelcome guests.

One morning, Maman Dlo heard someone singing above the water. When she crept closer to the surface to see who had disturbed her rest, she saw a young woman beating her laundry against a nearby rock. "Who sings so beautifully?" Maman Dlo asked in a raspy voice.

"Who is there?" the woman stuttered. "I am Ti Jeanne."
At these words, Maman Dlo rose from the water. The young woman was shocked by the sight of the water spirit, recognizing her immediately. Maman Dlo swayed from side to side on her serpent's tail as she spoke once more. "You are very beautiful, Ti Jeanne," she croaked.

The sound of the spirit's voice, accompanied by the swaying of her body, had a hypnotic effect on Ti Jeanne.

Slowly, Ti Jeanne began to wade into the river towards Maman Dlo. As she walked deeper into the water, the water spirit slapped her tail creating great waves that crashed over the young woman. Finally, when Ti Jeanne was submerged up to her nose, Maman Dlo spoke again. "You shall keep me company in the water, Ti Jeanne, and sing for me." Suddenly, with a wave of Maman Dlo's hand, Ti Jeanne's legs transformed into a long, shining fish's tail.

And so it was that Ti Jeanne went on to live for many years beneath the water with Maman Dlo, playing with the other river spirits and helping to watch over their home.

As Maman Dlo moved her tail in the water, waves washed over Ti Jeanne.

PRONUNCIATION:
GREEM-hild

CULTURE: Norse

BABA YAGA

PRONUNCIATION:
BA-ba ya-GA

CULTURE: Slavic

Baba Yaga is a witch in the Slavic folklore of eastern Europe. She lives in the forest in a magical house that has giant chicken's legs and can walk around on its own.

As well as being a witch, Grimhild is the Queen of Burgundy in Norse mythology. She has four children, two of whom she helped marry heroes using magic.

MEDEA

PRONUNCIATION:
meh-DEE-a

CULTURE:
Ancient Greek

Almost every region tells stories about witches, many of whom perform spells or brew potions. These women can be good, bad, or something in between, but they are always magical.

In ancient Greek myth, Medea is the princess of a land called Colchis. She is also a powerful witch who used her potion-making abilities to help the hero Jason.

WITCHES

MORGANA

PRONUNCIATION:
mor-GAH-na

CULTURE: Welsh

Morgana is a sorceress and possibly the half-sister of King Arthur – the legendary British ruler. Sometimes she uses her powers for good and at other times for evil.

LILITH

PRONUNCIATION:
LIH-lith

CULTURE:
Jewish and Mesopotamian

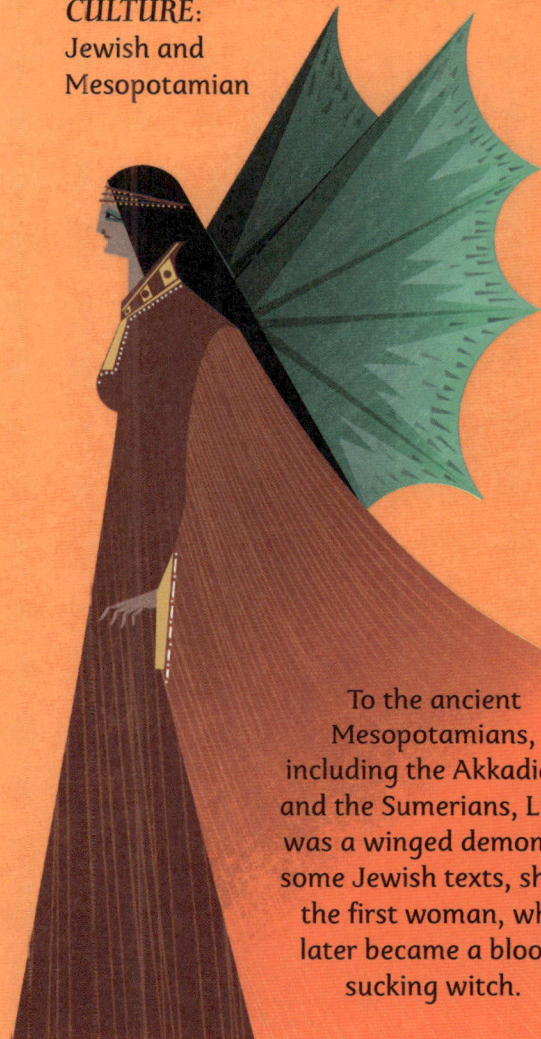

To the ancient Mesopotamians, including the Akkadians and the Sumerians, Lilith was a winged demon. In some Jewish texts, she is the first woman, who later became a blood-sucking witch.

LUTZELFRAU

PRONUNCIATION:
LOOTZ-el-frow

CULTURE:
German

Lutzelfrau is a legendary German witch. On Saint Lucy's Day, on 13 December, she visits the homes of children and gives gifts to those who are well behaved.

Baba Yaga's chores

Deep in the forest, there was a very unusual hut that stood on two spindly chicken's legs. This hut belonged to the witch Baba Yaga.

Baba Yaga had many powers. She loved nothing better than to fly through the trees in her giant mortar bowl with a pestle brandished in her hand. As she lived alone and rarely received visitors, a great many rumours were spread about her.

Some people even said she ate children for dinner.

Baba Yaga was therefore surprised to come home one day to discover a young woman standing in her hut with a doll in her hands. "Who are you?" the old woman growled.

"My apologies for the intrusion," the girl replied. "My name is Vasilisa, and my stepmother sent me to fetch fire from you."

Baba Yaga narrowed her eyes. "I see. Well, you can have the fire if you do some work for me. Clean my home, wash my clothes, and cook my dinner. If you fail, I shall eat you instead."

Vasilisa agreed, and the next morning, when Baba Yaga flew off to do whatever it is witches do, the girl set to work. However, it soon became clear that the chores were more than one person could manage. "What am to do?" Vasilisa wailed to her doll, which had been a gift from her birth mother.

"Don't cry, Vasilisa, cook the dinner and trust that all will be well," the doll replied.

Vasilisa stared at her doll in surprise, but seeing no other option, she did as the doll instructed. To her amazement, when dinner was done, she turned around to find the rest of the hut was spotless and the clothes had been hung out to dry.

Crying happy tears, she hugged her doll close.

Eventually, Baba Yaga returned, expecting a tasty dish of little girl but discovering instead that all the chores had been completed. "Out, get out," the witch yelled, annoyed she had been outwitted, "and take the fire with you." She grabbed a skull filled with fire and threw it at the girl.

Without hesitation, Vasilisa grabbed the skull and ran, her doll still held tightly to her chest.

Medea's magic

In the ancient land of Colchis, there lived a princess named Medea. Not only was she the daughter of the king, Aeëtes, she was also an incredibly powerful witch.

No one in all of Asia or Europe could compete with Medea's skills in potion-making. Yet still her father underestimated her — something he would come to regret.

One day, the citizens of Colchis spied an unfamiliar ship docking at the harbour. As they watched, countless sailors disembarked, led by a man dressed in richly embroidered clothes. This stranger, who must have been the crew's leader, asked the nearest Colchian to take him to the palace. And so it was that he arrived to meet with the king himself. "I am Aeëtes, king of this land," came Aeëtes' deep voice.

"King Aeëtes," the stranger replied. "I am Jason, captain of the Argo, and I have travelled all the way from Greece to ask you for the golden fleece."

Aeëtes smirked. The golden fleece, a woollen ram's coat made of pure gold, was his prized possession and Jason was not the first adventurer to come looking for it.

"Come dine with my family tonight, Jason, and we will discuss your request." Aeëtes replied.

That evening, Aeëtes and his family, including Medea, gathered in the great hall to feast with their guest. The princess was immediately intrigued by Jason. Little did she realize that the playful god of love, Eros, was preparing for some mischief. He had strung his bow and, hidden from sight, aimed it at the princess.

Without warning, Eros loosed an arrow and with expert precision struck Medea's heart.

Eros's arrows were no ordinary arrows, however. They caused their target to fall in love with whomever the person first saw. For Medea, this was Jason, and she talked to him all evening. Meanwhile, Aeëtes had a proposition. "Jason, I will allow you to have the fleece, but only if you are able to harness my bulls and sow the fields outside this palace with dragon's teeth."

The task sounded easy enough, so Jason agreed. Medea knew exactly the trick her father had planned though.

That evening, when Jason was resting by the fire, Medea snuck from her rooms to visit him.

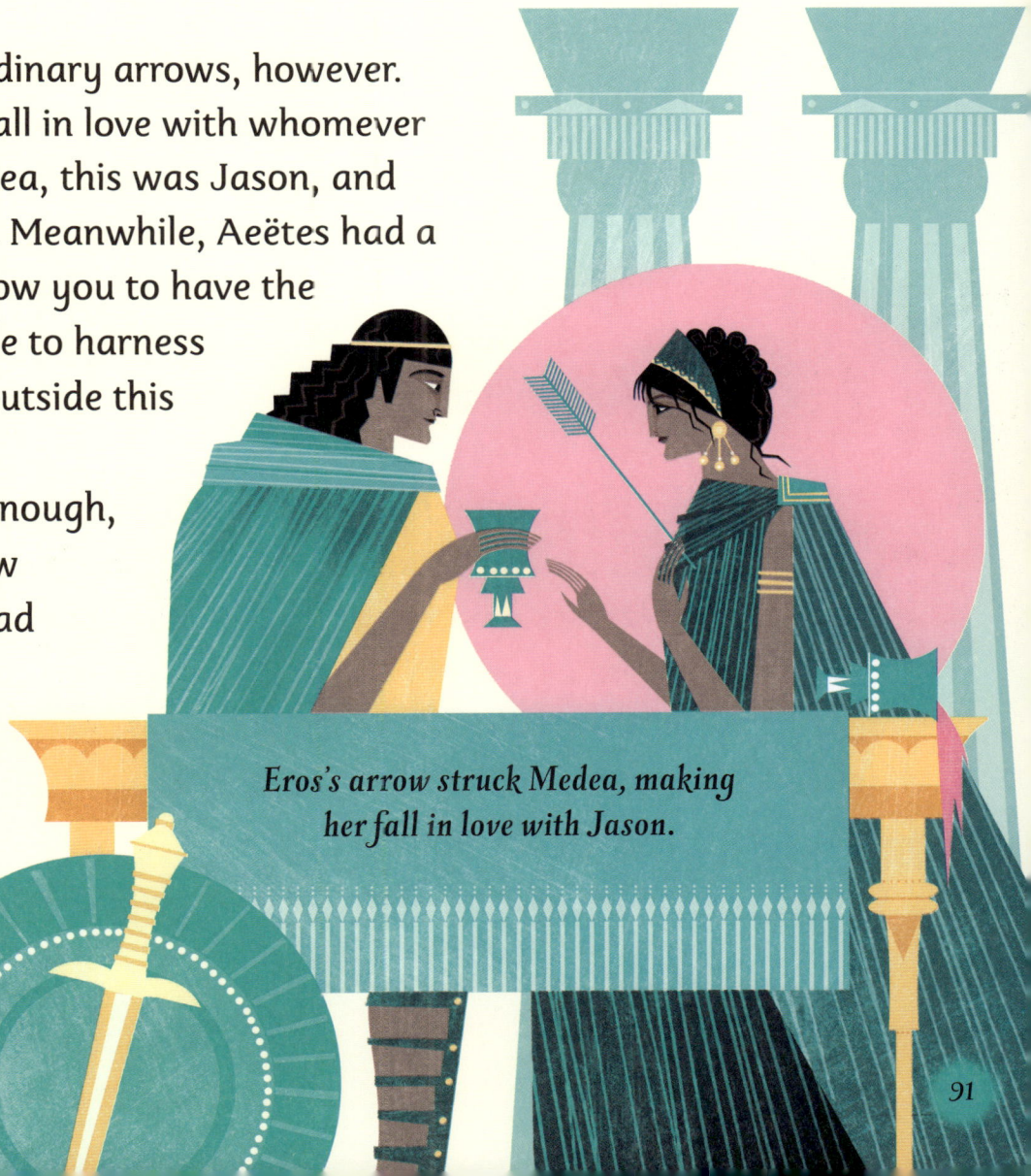

Eros's arrow struck Medea, making her fall in love with Jason.

"Jason," the princess whispered. "Be warned! The bulls breathe fire and when the dragon's teeth are planted, armed warriors will spring from the ground to attack you."

Jason was horrified. "Thank you for warning me, Medea, but why would you tell me this?" he asked.

"Because I love you and wish to run away with you. In exchange, I will help you complete my father's task," she replied, handing him a small bottle. "I brewed this potion myself and when spread on your shield and armour they will become indestructible to the bulls' fire. Then, when the warriors rise, you must throw a stone into their midst and they will fight each other instead."

Jason had fallen in love with Medea as well, and he promised to take her to Greece and make her his wife.

The next day, Jason followed Medea's instructions. With his magically protected armour and shield, he tied the bulls to a plough without being burned and then tricked the warriors into killing each other instead of him, just as Medea said they would.

Aeëtes' bulls blew plumes of fire at Jason as he approached them.

Aeëtes was furious that Jason had completed the task. He was sure Jason must have cheated, but he had no idea how. Not once did the king suspect his daughter. Determined to keep the golden fleece, he turned to Jason with a sly grin. "As promised, you may have the fleece – it is guarded by the dragon that lives in those caves." He pointed towards the Colchian mountains.

Jason had faced many monsters on his travels but never a dragon.

Medea, however, knew exactly what to do. They both journeyed to the caves and when they arrived, Medea released a potion into the air that sent the dragon into a deep sleep. No longer afraid he might be eaten by the beast, Jason grabbed the fleece. He and Medea then fled to his ship, where they set sail ready for their next adventure.

SHTRIGË

PRONUNCIATION:
SHTREE-g

CULTURE: Albanian

A shtrigë is a witch from Albanian folklore who drinks blood like a vampire. These witches fly around at night in the form of insects, such as flies and moths.

LOUHI

PRONUNCIATION:
LOH-ee

CULTURE: Finnish

In Finnish folklore, Louhi is a witch and the ruler of a land called Pohjola. Her powers give her the ability to shapeshift into various forms, including an eagle.

SADHBH

PRONUNCIATION:
SAHV

CULTURE: Irish

Sadhbh is a woman from Ireland who was twice turned into a deer by a resentful druid whom she refused to marry. While in human form, she fell in love with the hero Fionn, with whom she had a son, Oisín.

SHAPESHIFTERS

Throughout the folklore and legends of the world, there are women who can change their shape, although some are changed by the powers of others too. While these beings might appear human at first, they are often hiding an animal form underneath.

SELKIE

PRONUNCIATION: SEL-kee

CULTURE: Scottish

Selkies are creatures from Scottish legend who live in the sea. They take the form of seals in the water, but can take off their skins to reveal a human body.

LADY BAI

PRONUNCIATION: BAI

CULTURE: Chinese

Lady Bai is a figure in Chinese folklore who started out in life as a snake. Over thousands of years, she taught herself to transform into a woman.

KU-CHIN-DA-GAYYA

PRONUNCIATION: KOO CHIN DA GAI-a

CULTURE: Hausa

Ku-Chin-Da-Gayya is a shapeshifting woman from the folklore of the Hausa people from West and Central Africa. She is able to turn into various animals, including flies and birds.

KITSUNE

PRONUNCIATION: KIT-soo-nay

CULTURE: Japanese

Kitsune are magical creatures in Japanese legend that look like foxes, but which may have up to nine tails. They are also able to transform into humans and often become beautiful women.

95

Lady Bai's debt

There was once a tiny, white snake that lived at the bottom of a lake. One day, a hungry man was fishing in the lake and he was very happy when he caught the snake.

Luckily for the snake, however, another young man was watching and he took pity on the creature. He offered the hungry man a hundred copper coins in exchange for the tiny snake and then when the deal was done, he set it free once more.

Now, one thousand seven hundred years passed, and the snake practised the skill of transformation every day.

Over time, the snake grew larger and developed the ability to change into numerous different shapes, including that of a woman. In this form, she took the name Lady Bai. While the snake was in her human form, she was visited by the Golden Mother,

The Golden Mother appeared to Lady Bai.

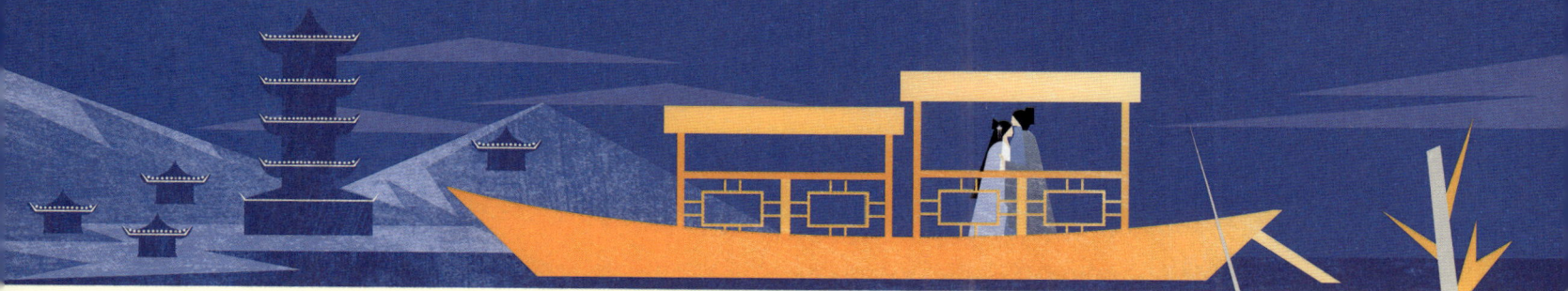

queen of the gods. "The man who saved your life so long ago has now been reborn and his name is Xu Xian. You must go to him and repay him for his kindness, for then you shall be able to join the gods," the Golden Mother told Lady Bai.

So, Lady Bai set off, and after a few days' travel she found the man named Xu Xian at Thunder Peak Pagoda. When Xu Xian saw her, he did not recognize her as the snake from his previous life, but he still offered her a lift on the boat he had rented. Lady Bai accepted and the two spent the journey chatting pleasantly.

To her surprise, Lady Bai quickly found herself falling in love with this generous and beautiful man.

Lady Bai's feelings, it turned out, were returned by Xu Xian and the two decided to marry. After a few years, Lady Bai discovered she was pregnant, and soon she gave birth to a baby boy. "What shall we name him?" asked Xu Xian.

"Before I gave birth, I dreamt that I was watched over by a mighty dragon," answered Lady Bai. "So let us call him Mengjiao." Xu Xian immediately approved of the name, which meant "to dream of dragons".

Lady Bai and Xu Xian fell in love and married.

After the birth of their son, Xu Xian received a visit from a monk named Fahai. Now, Fahai knew that Lady Bai was no ordinary woman and was determined to reveal her secret. "You have married a demon and I have come to capture her," Fahai said to Xu Xian, holding up a magical golden bowl.

Meanwhile, Lady Bai had come to see what was keeping her husband. When the golden bowl sensed her presence, it rose into the air and landed on her head. "Oh, the weight is too much," cried Lady Bai. "An entire mountain would be lighter."

*Slowly, she grew smaller and smaller
under the weight of the golden bowl.*

Xu Xian watched on horrified as the woman he loved disappeared, until only the golden bowl was left clattering on the floor. Quickly, he ran to snatch it up and discovered underneath a tiny, white snake.

"What have you done to my wife?" he wailed at Fahai.

Hearing the commotion, Xu Xian's sister Mrs Li came running just in time to witness Lady Bai's fate.

"What have you done to your wife?" she yelled. "Do not despair," the monk replied to the siblings. "Lady Bai was never human. Let me show you."

Fahai picked up the bowl and led the brother and sister to the banks of the river by Thunder Peak Pagoda.

Here, he laid down the vessel and from it rose the spirit of Lady Bai. "Husband, do not weep, for what Fahai says is true. I was sent to repay my debt to you from many centuries ago and now my time has come to leave the land of the mortals," she said.

Lady Bai's spirit then turned to her sister-in-law, "Please care for my son as if he were your own, and one day we will all be reunited again." With these words Lady Bai was gone, and although her family grieved her loss they remembered her always.

The spirit of Lady Bai rose up from the golden bowl.

99

The selkie's skin

*Once, a group of selkies had decided to swim
up to the shore to bask in the sun. These beings
looked like seals, but by removing their sealskins
they could take on human form.*

Meanwhile, a curious man was watching the selkies relaxing on the sand from behind a nearby rock. This young man was considered the most eligible bachelor in all of the Orkney Islands, but he had so far refused to marry. However, he found himself captivated by one of the selkie women he saw before him.

*Jumping from behind the rock, he startled the group, who all
snatched desperately for their sealskins and ran back into the sea.*

Unfortunately, the selkie woman had not been as quick as her friends and the stranger had grabbed her sealskin before she could reach it. The man knew that the selkie could not return to the sea

without her sealskin. "Please, I beg you, return my sealskin," the selkie pleaded.

"How about you become my wife instead?" the man said.

They went back and forth like this for some time until the selkie finally agreed to marry him. "What choice do I have?" she thought to herself.

For many years, the man and the selkie lived as husband and wife, and together they had seven children. One day, when her husband was out fishing, the selkie was caring for one of their daughters who had an injured foot. As the selkie moved around their home, she lamented that she could not find the thing she desired most.

"What are you looking for?" asked her daughter.

"A fine sealskin your father misplaced," replied her mother.

"Oh I know where that is," the girl said smiling. "One night, when father thought I was asleep, I saw him place it above your bed."

The selkie could not believe her luck. She ran to the bedroom and sure enough there the sealskin was hidden. Now, she loved her children dearly but she did not belong in this world. Immediately, she ran back to the shore, put on her sealskin, and returned to the sea, never to be seen again.

The young man grabbed the selkie's sealskin before she could return to the water.

Ku-Chin-Da-Gayya's sister

Ku-Chin-Da-Gayya lived with her family,
including her older sister. Now, her sister refused to
marry any man who asked her. Until one day,
two mysterious men arrived at their home.

These men were actually ghouls disguised as humans and
they were unlike any other men that Ku-Chin-Da-Gayya's sister
had met. This time, she was quick to agree to be the older
man's wife and they were married soon after.

Four days after the wedding, it was time for
Ku-Chin-De-Gayya's sister to leave the family home.

Ku-Chin-Da-Gayya, however, hated the thought
of being without her sister. "Let me come with you!"
she begged.
"I cannot take you with me," her sister
replied. "I don't even know where I'm going yet."
Ku-Chin-Da-Gayya was not to be put
off though. When the time came for the
newlyweds and the younger man to depart,
she transformed herself into a fly and hid
among her sister's things.

That night the three travellers set up camp together, completely unaware of Ku-Chin-Da-Gayya's presence. After they had settled down, the younger man approached his friend's wife. "Your husband demands that you bring us water," he commanded. With these words he stormed off back to his friend. Ku-Chin-Da-Gayya's sister had no idea where to find water nearby, however, and so she started to cry.

At the sound of her sister's sobs, Ku-Chin-Da-Gayya transformed back into herself and went to her sister.

"Behind that geza bush you will find some water," she told her sister. "What are you doing here?" her older sister asked in surprise. "I didn't want to leave you alone," Ku-Chin-Da-Gayya replied. Gratefully, her sister fetched the water and gave it to the two men. The next night, however, the younger man came to her again. "Your husband demands you bring us beans," he said.

Again her sister began to cry because it was the dry season and there were no beans to be found. But Ku-Chin-Da-Gayya knew what to do. "Gather the fruit from the geza bush, place it in a bowl, and cover it up. Then give the bowl to your husband," she said.

So, her sister did as she was told and when the men lifted the cover from the bowl, it revealed cooked beans!

Finally, the four travellers reached the home of the ghouls. The older man's family greeted them excitedly. They were very pleased that he had found himself a human wife, and even brought her sister, for humans were particularly tasty to ghouls. The first morning in their new village, Ku-Chin-Da-Gayya's sister sent her out with some food for her husband, who was working in the fields. Suspicious of the strange men, Ku-Chin-Da-Gayya first decided to fly overhead in the form of a bird to see what they were doing.

To her horror, Ku-Chin-Da-Gayya saw the men in their true form, bent over the ground eating frogs.

Ku-Chin-Da-Gayya realized immediately what her sister had married. Worse yet, she overheard their conversation and it was clear to her that the ghouls intended only death for both women.

Pretending nothing was amiss, Ku-Chin-Da-Gayya changed back into herself and then approached the men on foot. She delivered the food before hurrying back to the village. "Sister, your husband is a ghoul!" she whispered, not wishing to be overheard.

"This can't be," wailed her sister. "What shall we do?"

But Ku-Chin-Da-Gayya had a plan.

That night, when the ghouls were asleep, she took her sister's headdress and necklace and placed them on her sister's husband instead. A few hours later, his mother arrived.

Now, the mother ghoul planned to kill her son's wife so they could eat her the next day. It was dark, however, and she let her hands guide her. She felt the beads of the necklace and cloth of the headdress and slew her son by mistake.

When the Sun rose, it was clear what had happened and the mother ghoul was furious. Ku-Chin-Da-Gayya, meanwhile, bravely spoke up. "Eat your son if you like, but you shall not eat either of us," she said. And with those final words, she and her sister ran all the way back home.

MORTALS

The stories of remarkable mortal women have been retold for centuries, from the first women on Earth to legendary queens of ancient lands, and from brave warriors skilled in battle to storytellers who mesmerize with their gifts. While they may not have any magical powers, these women still manage impressive feats that make sure their tales continue to be told with each passing generation.

EMBLA

PRONUNCIATION:
EM-blah

CULTURE:
Norse

Embla is the first woman in Norse mythology. She was created by the gods from an elm tree at the same time as the first man, called Ask, was made from an ash tree.

FIRST WOMEN

In many cultures, the first humans to walk the Earth were a single man and woman. These people were created by gods, often from things in the natural world.

HINEAHUONI

PRONUNCIATION:
hih-nay-a-HOO-oh-nay

CULTURE:
Māori

In Māori belief, Hineahuone, which means "formed from the earth", is the first woman. She was made out of clay by Tāne-mahuta, the god of forests.

PANDORA

PRONUNCIATION:
pan-DOR-a

CULTURE:
Ancient Greek

Pandora is the first woman in ancient Greek mythology. She was created by the gods and sent to Earth with a jar full of all the world's ills to punish men, who had been given the secret of fire by the giant Prometheus.

UNGNYEO

PRONUNCIATION:
UNG-yo

CULTURE:
Korean

Ungnyeo, which means "bear woman" in Korean, was a bear who lived in a cave. Thanks to her dedication to the god Hwanung, she was transformed into the first woman.

EVE

PRONUNCIATION:
EEV

CULTURE: Christian, Islamic, and Jewish

Eve is the first woman in many religions. In Christianity and Judaism, she was created from the rib of Adam, the first man. They lived in a paradise, called the Garden of Eden, until they were banished for breaking the rules.

Pandora's gift

Zeus, king of the ancient Greek gods, was furious with humanity. Against his wishes, the giant Prometheus had given people the secret of fire.

Zeus believed that with fire, mortals would grow too powerful, and so he decided to bring chaos into their lives. He knew he would have to do so in secret, however, or else his trick might fail. So, one evening, Zeus set about devising a plan.

When Zeus was ready, he called the other gods and goddesses on Mount Olympus, their mountain home, to his chambers and asked them for their help. First, he turned to Hephaestus, god of craftsmanship. "I wish for you to make a female mortal," he said.

Hephaestus was surprised at Zeus' words, for all the humans that lived on Earth were men.

Still, Hephaestus nodded and set to work. When Hephaestus' job was done, Zeus turned to his daughter Athena, goddess of wisdom and war, and commanded, "Daughter, dress this woman in the finest silks and teach her the art of weaving."

And so, Athena did as her father asked. Then Zeus asked the messenger god Hermes to place a curious nature in the woman's heart. Finally, when Hermes had completed his task, Zeus stepped forward to look upon their creation.

"I shall name you Pandora, which means 'all gifts'. And you shall marry the giant Epimetheus," Zeus announced.

Pandora simply smiled, seeing no reason to argue. She followed Zeus to the home of her new husband, Epimetheus, who as it happened was also the brother of Prometheus. Before Zeus departed, however, he presented Pandora with a jar. "Take this as a wedding gift, Pandora," Zeus told her. "But remember never to open it."

Pandora frowned, but before she could ask why she could never open the jar, Zeus had vanished.

For a time, Pandora and Epimetheus lived happily enough as husband and wife and the jar went untouched. At the back of her mind, however, Pandora never forgot it was there. Every day, her curiosity grew as she wondered what could possibly be inside. This was exactly what Zeus had planned. The god knew that no human could resist the temptation of opening the jar forever. Finally, the day came when Pandora could wait no longer. She lifted the jar into her hands and pulled the stopper free. All at once Zeus' hopes were realized. For from the vessel streamed every horrible thing that could possibly be imagined.

Out into the world spilled plague, drought, famine, and war, flooding the once peaceful Earth with evil.

As soon as Pandora saw what had been inside the jar, she knew Zeus had played a cruel trick. Before anything else escaped, she resealed the jar, trapping the final thing that Zeus had placed inside – hope.

With this one thing kept safe inside the jar, quick-thinking Pandora had ensured that no matter how terrible times were or what awful events might happen, people would always have hope.

Pandora put the lid back on the jar as fast as she could, stopping hope from escaping.

Ungnyeo's patience

There was once a bear and a tiger that lived together in a cave. Every day, they prayed to Hwanung, the god who looked after people, to turn them into humans.

Hwanung was impressed by the bear and the tiger's dedication, and one day he appeared to them in the form of a man. The animals watched as he proceeded to take out twenty cloves of garlic and a sprig of wormwood. "Eat these and remain out of the daylight for one hundred days," Hwanung told them. "If you manage this, then you shall be human."

Hwanung offered garlic and wormwood to the bear and tiger.

So, the bear and the tiger did as the god had instructed. They ate his gifts and for the following weeks tried their hardest to avoid the sun. On the twenty-first day, however, the tiger could bear it no longer and left their cave.

The bear, meanwhile, was more patient and was rewarded by being transformed into a woman, named Ungnyeo.

Although pleased to be human, Ungnyeo was also lonely. She longed for a child and a family of her own. One day, she sat down beneath a holy tree and prayed again to Hwanung, hoping he would remember her from before.

Hwanung did indeed remember Ungnyeo and his heart was moved by her prayers. In fact, he was so struck by her determination that he offered to marry her himself. So, the two were wed and together had a son named Dangun Wanggeom, who would one day found the first kingdom in Korea.

Ungnyeo became a woman and married the god Hwanung.

QUEENS

Legendary queens are said to have ruled over some of the earliest cities and civilizations. Whether they did so alone or alongside a king, they were powerful figures.

ISOLDE

PRONUNCIATION: IH-zol-duh

CULTURE: Irish

Princess Isolde is the legendary daughter of the king and queen of Ireland. She became queen when she married King Mark of Cornwall, but her heart always belonged to the hero Tristan.

DRAUPADI

PRONUNCIATION: DROW-pa-dee

CULTURE: Hindu

Draupadi is the legendary queen of the ancient city of Indraprastha in India through her husband, King Arjuna. He was only one of her husbands, however, as she was married to his four brothers as well.

SIGRID

PRONUNCIATION: SIG-reed

CULTURE: Norse

In Norse mythology, more than one king asked Sigrid the Haughty for her hand in marriage, but she chose to wed King Erik the Victorious of Sweden. She was well known for her wisdom.

ALCESTIS

PRONUNCIATION: al-SEST-iss

CULTURE: Ancient Greek

In ancient Greek mythology, Alcestis is queen of the city of Pherae. She sacrificed her life for her husband, Admetus, but because of her loyalty was allowed to return from the underworld.

DIDO

PRONUNCIATION: DAI-doh

CULTURE: Ancient Roman

In ancient Roman myth, Dido is the founder of Carthage in northern Africa. She asked a local ruler for just enough land that could be covered by an ox's hide, but she cut the hide into strips to make a large circle and so built the city.

QUEEN OF SHEBA

PRONUNCIATION: SHEE-ba

CULTURE: Christian, Islamic, and Jewish

The Queen of Sheba is the legendary ruler of the ancient realm of Sheba. She is known for bringing many priceless gifts to King Solomon, ruler of the Kingdom of Israel.

Alcestis's sacrifice

Alcestis was the queen of a city called Pherae, where she ruled alongside her husband, King Admetus.

The two had been married for many years when Admetus became gravely ill. It was soon clear to anyone who saw him that he had just days to live. Yet, there was still a chance he might be saved. This was because the god Apollo had once blessed the king with an opportunity to escape death – though this would come at a price.

If someone were to willingly give their own life in exchange for Admetus's, then the king could live on.

However, no one wanted to die in Admetus's place. Not those he had risked his own life for in the past, not even his parents. Everyone shrank back from the prospect except one, his wife Alcestis.

Alcestis and Admetus loved each other very much and the queen could not imagine life without her husband. Admetus begged his wife not to give up her own life for his but she could not be persuaded. "Our people still need you," she stated firmly. "And some day, I will see you again."

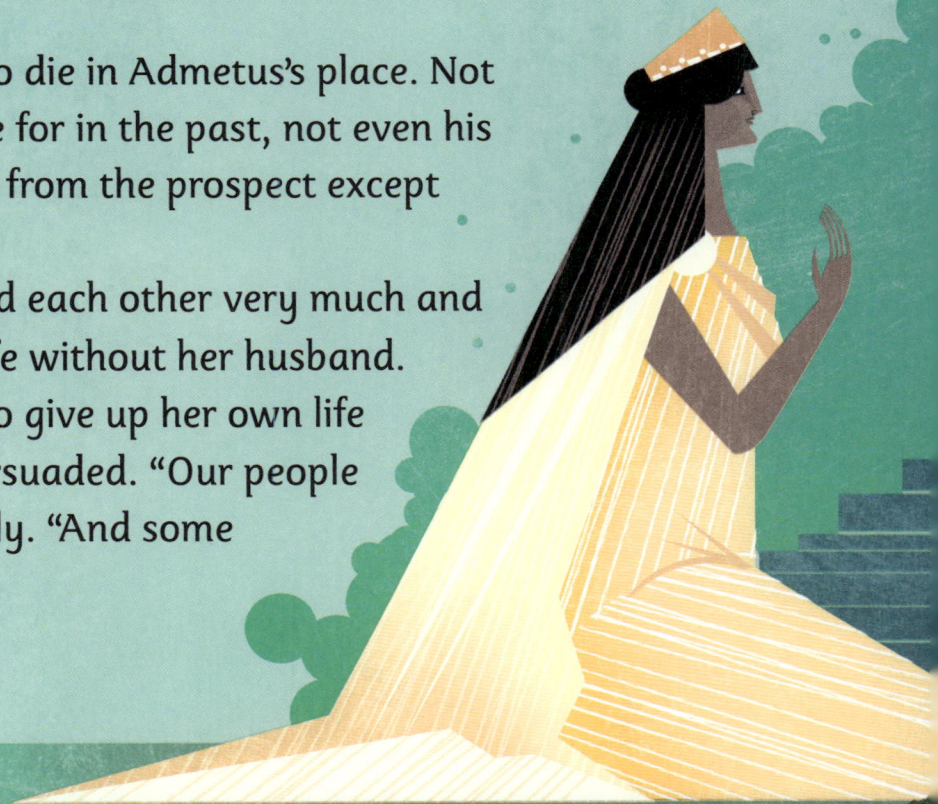

Persephone was moved by Alcestis's love for her husband.

Before she could be stopped, Alcestis had called to the gods to take her away in place of Admetus. As Apollo had promised, they did just that and the queen travelled deep into the depths of the underworld.

There, she met the queen of the underworld, Persephone.

Persephone had been listening to Alcestis and Admetus on Earth and the idea of them being separated made her sad. The goddess was so moved by Alcestis' sacrifice that she could not bear to let the woman enter the underworld so soon. "No, Alcestis, return to Earth and be with your husband," she said. "Your sacrifice has been acknowledged and Admetus will live but so will you, until you are both old and grey."

And so Alcestis and Admetus were reunited and ruled Pherae together till the end of their days.

Draupadi's husbands

Draupadi was the daughter of King Drupada, but she was not born in the usual way. Her father, hoping for a powerful son to defeat his enemies, burned offerings to the gods on a sacred fire, but Draupadi sprang from the flames.

When Draupadi had grown up, her father organized a contest to help her choose a husband. In order to win the princess's hand, a suitor had to fire an arrow through the eye of a fish made from gold, with only the target's reflection in a pool of water to help him aim.

Archer after archer attempted the feat without success until finally a man named Arjuna took his turn. Arjuna was one of the five Pandava brothers, along with Yudhishthira, Bhuma, Nakula, and Sahadeva.

Arjuna pulled back the string on his bow, stared into the pool, and let loose an arrow, striking the fish's eye right in the middle.

Draupadi had found her husband! The other unsuccessful suitors, however, were jealous and they attacked Arjuna and Draupadi. It took the help of all four of Arjuna's brothers to help beat the men back. Together, they all escaped and ran back home. "Mother, guess what I found today," Arjuna shouted as they arrived.

"Whatever it is make sure to share it with your brothers as I taught you," his mother shouted back, not realizing that Arjuna was referring to his future wife. The brothers did not know what to do for they always did what their mother told them to.

Draupadi, meanwhile, merely smiled. "You are all brave warriors, and I shall happily be a wife to each of you," she said. And so it was that Draupadi found herself with five husbands instead of one.

Life with five husbands was not always smooth sailing. On one occasion, Yudhishthira was playing dice with another prince named Duryodhana. Yudhishthira was losing badly. He had already bet his kingdom, and next he offered up himself for the following roll of the dice. Once again, Duryodhana won the game and Yudhishthira held up his hands to say he had nothing left to bet. "You have your wife, Draupadi, do you not?" Duryodhana replied.

Desperate and careless, Yudhishthira accepted Duryodhana's suggestion. To his horror, Yudhishthira's luck remained as bad as before and he watched as the dice rolled in Duryodhana's favour.

When Draupadi learned that one of her husbands had lost her in a game of dice, she was furious.

Nevertheless, she was made to follow Duryodhana's brother, Dushasana, to the winner's court. "How dare you think to win me in a game of dice?" Draupadi demanded immediately upon her arrival. "What right does Yudhishthira have to bet me? Not only had Yudhishthira already lost himself in the game, but I am queen in my own right."

Dushasana pulled at Draupadi's sari, but as she spun, more fabric kept appearing.

Sympathetic to Draupadi's words, another of Duryodhana's brothers, a man named Vikarna, turned to the court. "In your judgement, is Draupadi right?" he asked. The answer was immediate: Draupadi was correct! No one had the right to bet a woman: not her husband, her father, or even her gods.

This angered Duryodhana and he ordered his brother, Dushasana, to remove Draupadi's clothes to shame her. When Dushasana tried to grab the cloth of the sari that Draupadi wore, however, she called to the god Krishna for his protection.

No matter how Dushasana tugged and pulled at her clothing, there was always more material, and soon the man grew too exhausted to carry on.

It was at that moment that Duryodhana's parents, the king and queen, suddenly arrived. They were shocked by the actions of their sons. "Release this woman at once," the queen demanded.

"How can we make it up to you Draupadi?" asked the king.

"All I want is freedom for my husband and me," Draupadi answered. Her wish was granted, and so she saved both herself and Yudhishthira from the clutches of Duryodhana.

Isolde's sorrow

There once lived a young princess of Ireland named Isolde. Her beauty was known of far and wide, so much so that King Mark of Cornwall decided that he wanted her as his wife.

The king had too many duties, however, to go and ask Isolde for her hand himself, so in his place he sent the knight Tristan, whom he trusted above all others. Tristan set sail and soon arrived on the shores of Ireland, but before he could travel to find Isolde, he was met with a dangerous task.

Tristan learned that there was a dragon nearby that was terrorizing the local people.

Braver and possibly more foolish than most, Tristan decided he would slay the terrible beast. He took his sword and shield and climbed to the dragon's lair. Tristan battled the dragon and succeeded in killing it, but in the process he was terribly injured.

Wounded and exhausted, Tristan fell down unconscious. Another man, meanwhile, had been watching and saw an opportunity for himself. He lopped off the dragon's head and, without a second look at Tristan, carried it to the king. "I have slain the dragon that terrorized our land," he declared. "Won't you let me marry your daughter Isolde for my victory?"

The king enthusiastically agreed, but Isolde was more suspicious. She knew the man to be a coward and so the next day she took two friends and rode on horseback to the place where the dragon had been defeated.

There, Isolde spotted Tristan's body and knew immediately this must be the man who had saved them all.

Bending over the hero, Isolde was relieved to discover he was still breathing. She quickly ferried him back to the castle to her mother, the queen, with the help of her friends. "This is the man who really killed the dragon," she explained. "Can you heal him?"

The queen was very skilled in healing and she set about tending to the young man. After a few days, Tristan awoke, both surprised to be alive and to have ended up in Isolde's home.

The skillful queen healed Tristan.

When Isolde asked Tristan who he was, he explained the reason that had brought him to Ireland. On learning the news, the king was angry at the man who had lied, but wholeheartedly agreed to the engagement between Isolde and King Mark.

A date was set for Isolde to depart with the knight, but before they left her mother brewed a special potion.

This mixture would ensure that the newlyweds fell in love. The queen gave the love potion to Isolde's companion Brangein, who was to travel to Cornwall too, and told her to pour it into the couple's drinks after the wedding.

So, the party set sail. However, during the voyage, Tristan found the potion where Brangein had hidden it. Thinking it was an ordinary bottle of wine, he shared it with Isolde and they instantly fell in love.

Tristan and Isolde spent every moment they could together on the journey, but when they arrived in Cornwall, Isolde had no choice but to marry King Mark. Still, their feelings refused to go away. They would meet each night in the garden to spend time with one another.

Unfortunately, their meetings did not go unnoticed.

King Mark summoned the pair and asked them if they were in love. Though they both denied it, he did not believe them. Tristan was banished from the realm and told never to see Isolde again.

And for many years Tristan and Isolde did not set eyes on one another.

One day, however, Tristan fell gravely ill. He was now married himself, but he had never truly forgotten Isolde. When he realized he was dying, he sent for the Queen of Cornwall to try and heal him.

At the messenger's request, Isolde immediately set out, for she too still felt the same love for Tristan. When she arrived, however, it was too late. Tristan had already passed away. Her heart broken beyond repair, Isolde lay down beside him and died in his arms.

The pair were buried side by side, and from their graves a magnificent tree grew as a symbol of their eternal love.

A great tree grew up above the graves of Tristan and Isolde.

There are tales of legendary warriors wielding swords and fighting daring battles from around the world. Many of these characters are women with skills unmatched by any other.

WARRIORS

PRONUNCIATION: BREEN-hild

CULTURE: Norse

In Norse mythology, Brynhild is one of the Valkyries – a group of warrior women who serve the god Odin and goddess Freya. They guide fallen soldiers to the afterlife.

URDUJA

PRONUNCIATION: er-DOO-ha

CULTURE: Philippine

Urduja is a legendary Philippine warrior princess who ruled a land called Kaylukari. She led her own army and refused to marry anyone who could not defeat her in combat.

ATALANTA

PRONUNCIATION:
at-a-LAN-ta

CULTURE: Ancient Greek

Atalanta is a huntress, runner, and wrestler in ancient Greek mythology. She was abandoned in the forest as a baby, but was rescued by a bear and grew up to become the greatest archer in the land.

SCÁTHACH

PRONUNCIATION:
SKA-hahk

CULTURE: Irish

Scáthach is an expert fighter in Irish myth who lives on the Isle of Skye in Scotland. She taught many great warriors their skills, including the hero Cú Chulainn, and could predict the future.

MULAN

PRONUNCIATION: MOO-lan

CULTURE: Chinese

In Chinese legend, Mulan is a woman who joined the emperor's army disguised as a man so that her father did not have to fight. She became a celebrated warrior.

129

Mulan's secret

Long ago, there lived a young woman in China named Mulan. She was the eldest of her parents' three children and they could not ask for a more loyal daughter.

Mulan loved her family dearly and this was why, when news came that the emperor was summoning troops to fight a dangerous enemy, she began to worry. When she read the list of soldiers who were to join the army, Mulan saw with horror her father's name written there. "My father is no longer a young man, he is frail and surely won't survive," she cried. "And I do not have a brother old enough to take his place."

It was the thought of an older brother that gave Mulan an idea, however.

Hurrying from her home, Mulan headed to the eastern market and there she bought a horse. Then she made her way to the western market where she bought a saddle. Next, she stopped by the southern market to buy a bridle, before finally arriving at the northern market where she bought a whip. With her horse fully equipped, Mulan swapped her clothes for armour and set off from home.

Mulan had decided that she would take her father's place in the army. All she had to do was pretend to be a man.

Mulan travelled for many days, across the river and over the mountains, until finally she found the army. Dodging between the soldiers, she found their commander and added her name to the ranks.

For ten years, Mulan fought bravely alongside her fellow soldiers.

She grew to be as strong as the strongest of them, as fast as the fastest of them, and as agile as the most agile of them. Not once did anyone suspect that she was not the man she said she was.

Finally, the day came when the war was won, and Mulan, along with her fellow soldiers, was summoned to the palace of the emperor. He was supremely grateful for their service and wanted to thank them in whatever way he could. "I have heard of your great courage from far and wide young man, and I would like to offer you a place in my court," he said to Mulan.

"I am honoured by your offer, but all I want is to return home to my family," she replied. The emperor nodded.

"There must be something I can give you for your service though?" he asked.

"All I ask is for a horse that can run a thousand miles so I might travel fast and safely," Mulan said.

The emperor had one of his finest horses brought to Mulan that very evening. And so she set out on her journey, back over the mountains and across the river. When Mulan arrived home, it was her parents who were the first to spy her galloping in. "Mother, Father. It is me!" she cried, jumping from her horse. "Mulan."

"Surely not," her mother gasped. But as the young soldier came closer, she finally recognized her daughter's face. The family hugged one another tightly before they led Mulan inside so she could tell them all about her time at war.

The next day, Mulan left her home dressed in the clothes she had worn long ago.

As she walked through the town, she spotted a group of her fellow soldiers who had returned not long after her. When she approached them, however, it was clear they did not realize who she was. "It's me, Mulan," she laughed.

"So it is," one man cried. "But Mulan, you are a woman, yet you fought so bravely by our side."

Mulan laughed again. "It seems men and women are not so very different when they fight side by side."

Brynhild's true love

Brynhild was a Valkyrie, a brave warrior who served the gods. She spent her days happily battling her foes, until one day she accidentally angered the king of the gods, Odin.

During a fight, Brynhild defended a man called Agnar, but Odin had wished Agnar to be defeated. As punishment for saving Agnar, Odin placed a curse upon Brynhild. "You shall never again be victorious in battle. You will instead have to marry," Odin declared.

"I will only marry a man without fear," replied Brynhild defiantly, before Odin put her into an enchanted sleep. Odin then placed her body in a tower, and as he did so roaring fires sprang up around the building.

For a long time Brynhild slumbered undisturbed, until the hero Sigurd made it into the tower.

"It is time to awaken," Sigurd said when he discovered her.
"Who has awoken me?" Brynhild asked him suspiciously. The two warriors talked for hours and Sigurd listened raptly as Brynhild shared her wisdom. Finally, he asked if she would be his wife, and Brynhild agreed.

Brynhild lay asleep in the tower, guarded by flames.

Before they could wed, however, Sigurd had to journey to the court of Queen Grimhild, promising to return for Brynhild. Now, Grimhild was also a witch, and she wanted Sigurd to marry her daughter, Gudrun. When Sigurd arrived, Queen Grimhild gave him a potion that made him forget his love for Brynhild and instead agree to marry Gudrun.

Meanwhile, Grimhild's son Gunnar, having heard of Brynhild's skills, now wished to marry her. However, only Sigurd was able to cross the flames around her tower. Luckily for Gunnar, Sigurd was happy to help.

Using magic, Sigurd disguised himself as Gunnar
and returned to Brynhild through the fire.

The fake Gunnar explained to Brynhild that Sigurd was no longer in love with her and said that she should marry him instead. Brynhild was sad, but agreed, so the two married and together they left the tower.

Once Brynhild and the real Gunnar were united, however, Gudrun revealed Sigurd's trick to her. Brynhild was outraged. "I will never truly be your wife unless Sigurd is dead," she said to Gunnar.

Gunnar did not want to lose Brynhild, so he attacked and killed Sigurd. But at the terrible news of his death, Brynhild was overcome with grief and regretted what she had done. To Gunnar's horror, she brought a sword to her chest and took her own life, having lost her true love.

PRONUNCIATION:
sa-LOH-mee

CULTURE:
Christian

SIM CHEONG

PRONUNCIATION:
SHIM CHONG

CULTURE:
Korean

Salome is the stepdaughter of King Herod Antipas in the New Testament of the Bible. He granted her anything she wanted after she danced well at his birthday.

Sim Cheong is a woman from Korean legend who looked after her blind father. She sacrificed herself by jumping into the ocean to restore his eyesight, but was rescued by the god of the sea.

It wasn't just queens and warriors who left their mark on the world. Some legendary women are remembered for their actions. From dancing to weaving and from healing to storytelling, their skills were all different, but extraordinary.

ARTISTS, PERFORMERS, AND HEALERS

SHAHRAZAD

PRONUNCIATION:
sha-ha-ra-ZAD

CULTURE: Sasanian

In the collection of tales called One Thousand and One Nights, Shahrazad is a Sasanian storyteller. Her husband, the king, killed his wife each day, but Shahrazad told a new story each night to stay alive. The Sasanian Empire was found in and around ancient Iran.

ARACHNE

PRONUNCIATION:
a-RAK-nee

CULTURE: Ancient Greek

Arachne is a weaver in ancient Greek mythology. She claimed to be as good as Athena, the goddess of weaving herself. After they both wove a tapestry, Athena turned Arachne into a spider.

ELAINE OF ASTOLAT

PRONUNCIATION:
eh-LAYN of A-stoh-lat

CULTURE:
British

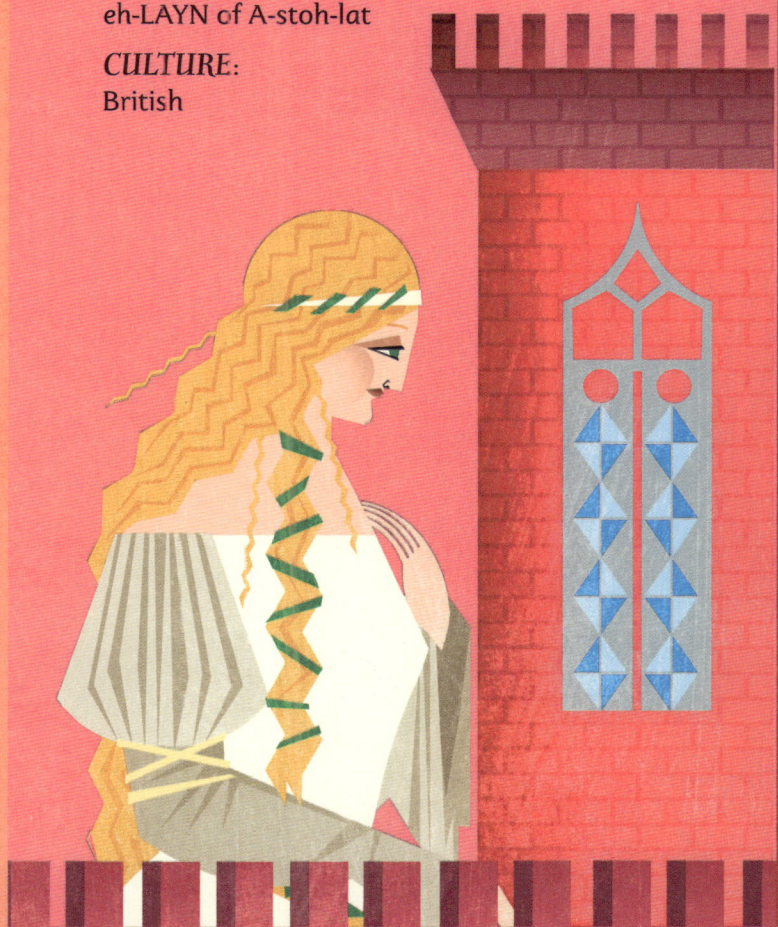

A noblewoman from Arthurian legend, Elaine of Astolat fell in love with the knight Lancelot. She healed him when he was wounded, but passed away when he refused to marry her.

Shahrazad's tales

A long time ago, there lived a young woman named Shahrazad who was the daughter of King Shahryar's chief advisor, or vizier. Her greatest joy was reading.

Shahrazad read anything she could. History books, collections of myths, and tales of past rulers and heroes. No one who met her doubted that she knew more stories than anyone else in the kingdom.

The king, meanwhile, was a miserable man. His wife had run away and left him, so he had decided to marry a new woman every morning only to have her killed the next day.

The king's people feared him rather than loved him, but no one knew how to end his reign of violence.

Finally, one day, Shahrazad went to her father with a request. "I wish you to offer me to the king as his new wife," she said, for she could no longer watch as so many other women were sacrificed.

The vizier pleaded with his daughter to let someone else go in her place. However,

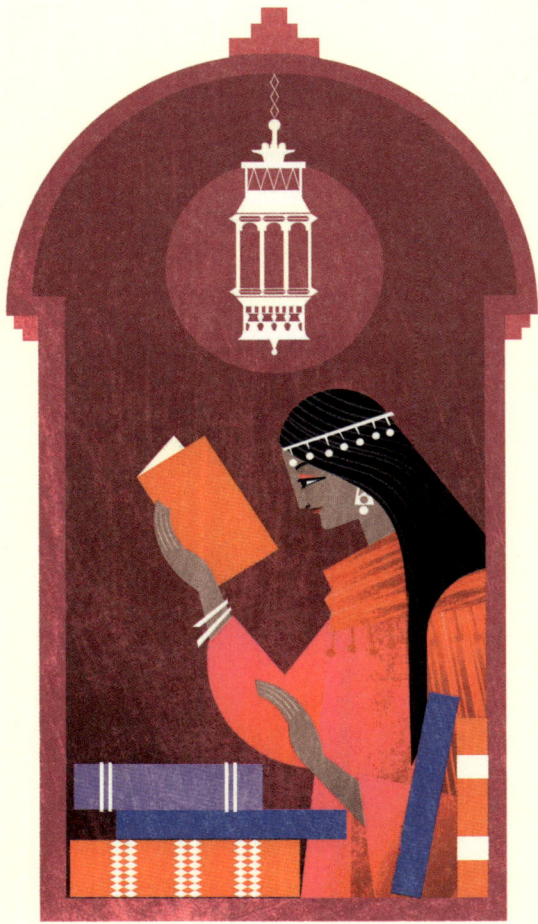

Shahrazad's mind was made up, for she had a plan. Before she was taken to the king for their wedding, she went to visit her sister Dunyazad. "Sister," Shahrazad began. "Tonight I will ask the king to allow you to visit me, as it is my last night on Earth. If he allows it, do one thing when you arrive. Request that I tell a story."

Despite her sister's questions, Shahrazad wouldn't say anything more. Brushing aside a tear, Shahrazad hugged her sister goodbye and departed together with her father for the palace.

The wedding was small and over quickly, and soon enough Shahrazad was left alone with the king.

"Husband, will you allow my sister to visit me on this final evening?" she asked. The king saw no reason to object and so Dunyazad was sent for.

When the younger woman arrived, she quickly obeyed her sister's instructions and said, "Oh, Shahrazad, please will you tell us one of your stories, if the king permits?" She turned to King Shahryar, "You may have heard that my sister here is the finest storyteller in all the land."

The king enjoyed a story as much as the next person and so, with a nod of consent, settled down to listen to Shahrazad's tale.

The tale began with a merchant and a mischievous spirit called a djinn. Shahrazad narrated the story with enthusiasm and flair, speaking long into the night. The first story turned into a second, but before she could tie up the ending, the Sun had already risen.

As dawn broke, Shahrazad ceased her tale, leaving her small audience with countless questions.

"But I must hear the rest!" Dunyazad insisted.

"I would need another night to have time to finish the tale," Shahrazad explained.

"Then another night you will have," declared the king, for he too was desperate to find out what happened next.

And so, in this way, Shahrazad lived another day. When the second night came, she took up her story once more only to find that it led to the start of another adventure.

When the Sun rose in the morning, the story was not yet complete again.

So engrossed was the king in the stories that each night he granted Shahrazad another day so that he could carry on listening to her. As the days passed, he found himself enthralled by both the tales the young woman spun and also by Shahrazad herself.

When the thousand and first night arrived since their marriage, the king sat down eagerly and waited for the next tale to begin. "I'm sorry to say I have no more stories left to tell," said Shahrazad. "My life is in your hands."

The king knew immediately what Shahrazad meant. He could not imagine a night without his wife, however. It seemed King Shahryar had fallen in love with the clever storyteller. "Beloved wife, that does not matter," replied Shahryar. "Let us go to sleep beside one another tonight, and for every night until we are both old and grey."

And this was how Shahrazad ended the fear and horror that had once controlled her kingdom.

Shahrazad told one captivating tale after another to her husband and sister.

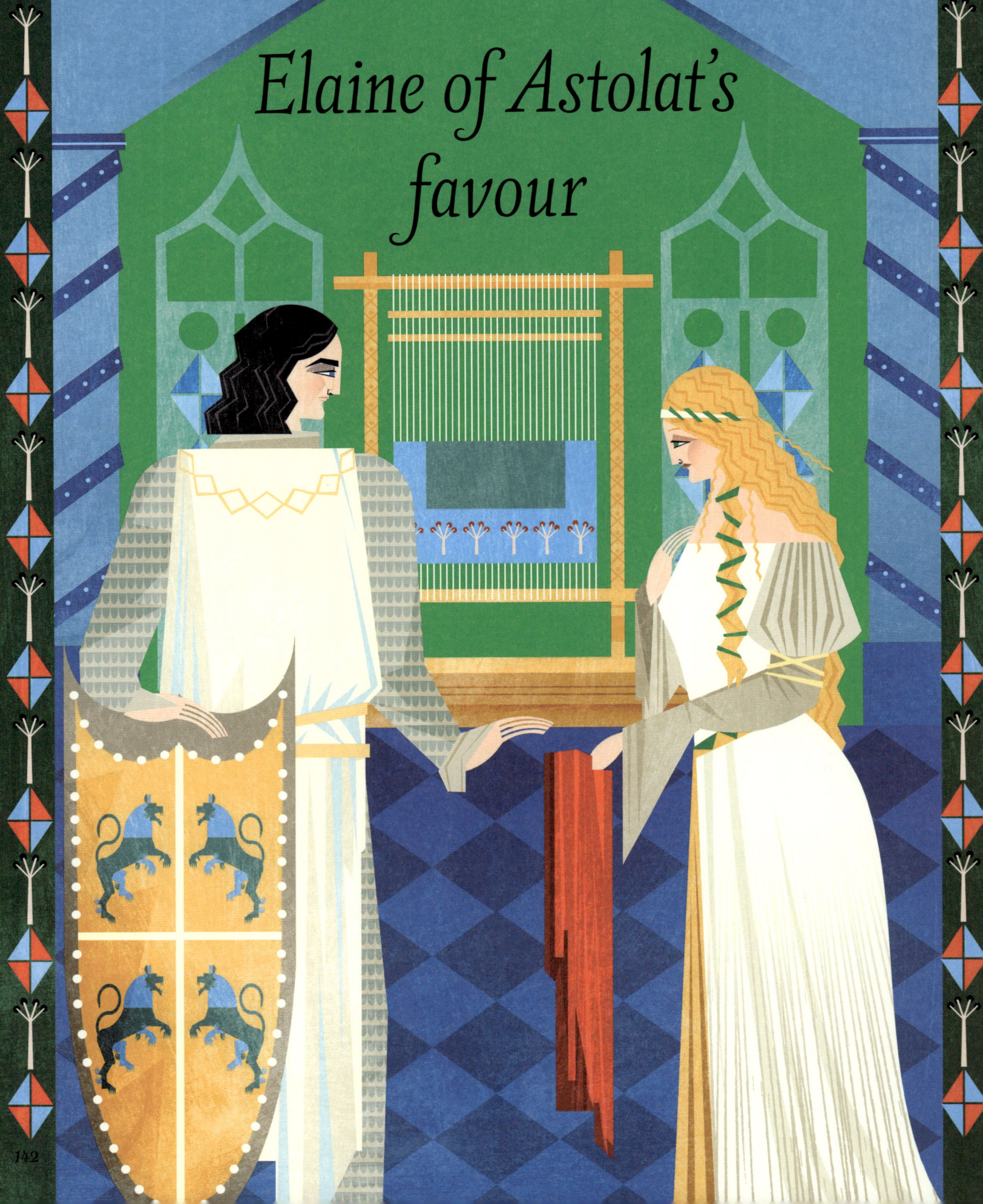

Elaine of Astolat's favour

There was once a noblewoman named Elaine who lived in the castle of Astolat with her family. She often passed her days alone, weaving elaborate tapestries in her room. That was until Sir Lancelot visited her home.

Sir Lancelot was a knight of King Arthur's court, and he had stopped by to see his friend, who happened to be Elaine's brother. As soon as Elaine spied Lancelot, she was struck by a deep and all-consuming love for this mysterious knight.

Now, Lancelot was going to participate in the local jousting tournament and Elaine hoped to offer him a lucky token, or favour, for the contest. Summoning her courage, she went to speak to the knight. "Will you accept this sleeve from me to keep beside you when you ride?" she asked, holding out a sleeve of rich red fabric.

"Gladly, my lady," answered Lancelot.

Lancelot did not, however, wish anyone to see that he carried Elaine's favour, for he was in love with someone else.

The knight took the shield he usually carried and asked Elaine to keep it safe for him. With his helmet on, and without his shield, Lancelot knew he would not be recognized.

The next day, Lancelot rode his horse in the tournament and defeated every opponent that he faced. During the jousting, however, he was wounded badly. So, Elaine's brother took him to see a healer.

Meanwhile, the knight Gawaine had come to Astolat, curious to try and find out who the nameless knight was that had defeated everyone so easily. When he asked Elaine, she said simply, "It must be the man I love!"

"But what is his name?" asked the knight.

"That I do not know, but I can show you the shield he left with me," she replied, fetching it for Gawaine. Upon seeing the shield, Gawaine immediately recognized the emblem of his friend Lancelot.

"Oh, but this is terrible, my lady." Gawaine exclaimed, "For the knight is my friend Lancelot. He was wounded and may not survive."

Elaine was horrified at this news and begged her father to let her go and find Lancelot.

When he agreed, she mounted her horse and set off on her quest. Finally, after hours of riding, she spotted her brother outside the healer's home and knew Lancelot must be inside. Leaping from her horse, she hurried into the hut and found Lancelot upon the bed.

"My love!" she cried running to him. Lancelot smiled at Elaine and kissed her on the cheek.

For the next few months, Elaine remained by Lancelot's side. Day and night she

Elaine carefully nursed the injured Lancelot back to health.

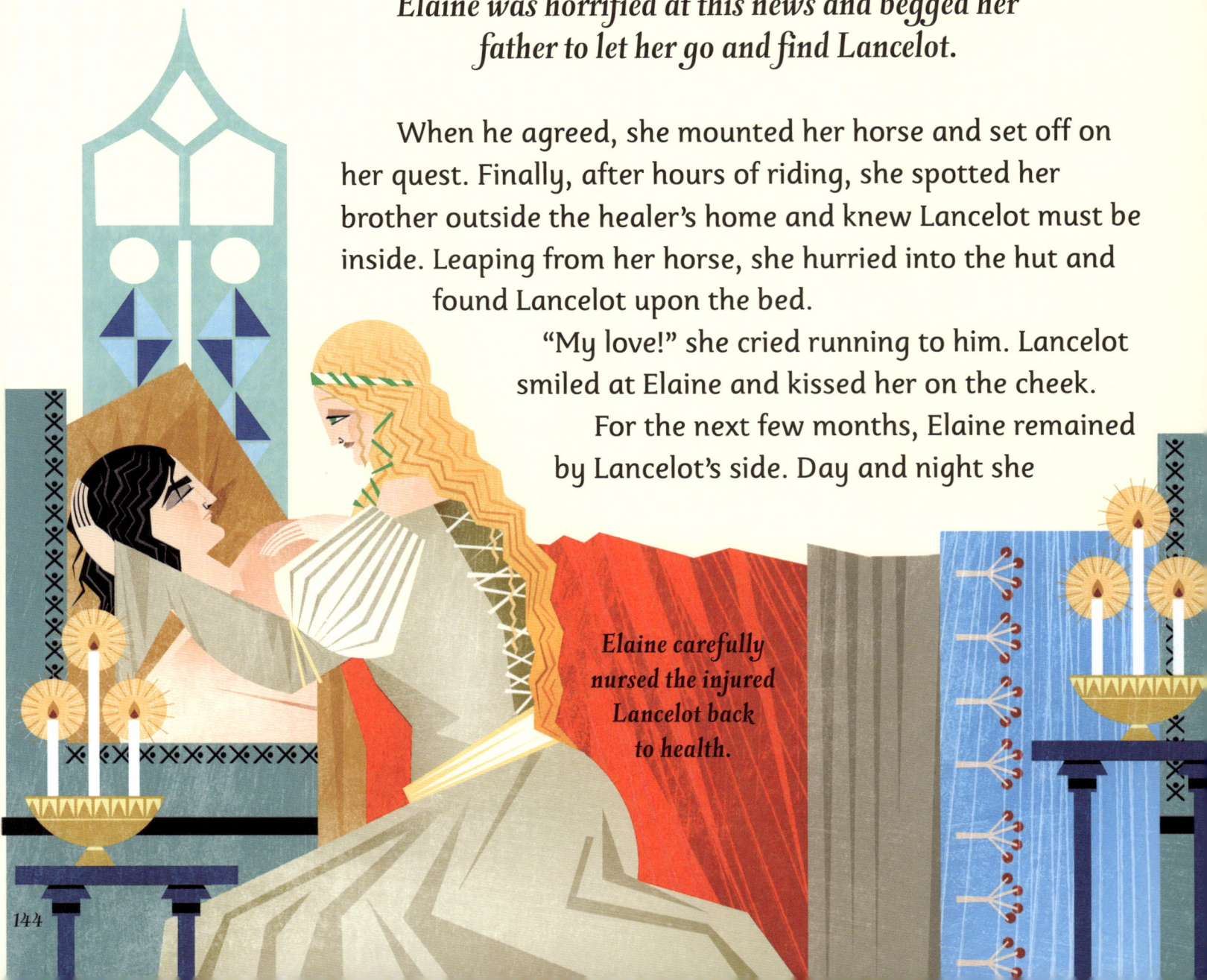

tended to him in his sickbed, bringing him food and drink, her commitment never wavering.

Finally, when Lancelot was recovered, they returned together to Astolat. "I love you with all my soul," Elaine told him when they had arrived. "Will you be my husband now that you are well?"

"I cannot, my lady, for I do not plan ever to wed," Lancelot replied carelessly. "But I will gift you one thousand pounds every year for your kindness."

Elaine was shocked by this offer, for she had stayed with him for love not money.

Elaine was so overwhelmed with sadness that she had to be taken to her chambers to lie down. For the next ten days, she could not sleep, eat, or drink. Eventually, she became too weak to lift her head and she could request only one last thing of her father. "Write my story down on a sheet of parchment," she asked. "And when I depart this world, place my body on a boat so I may sail away on the River Thames." Then she was gone. Devastated, her family did as she asked, and Elaine floated down the river with the story of her love clutched in her hand.

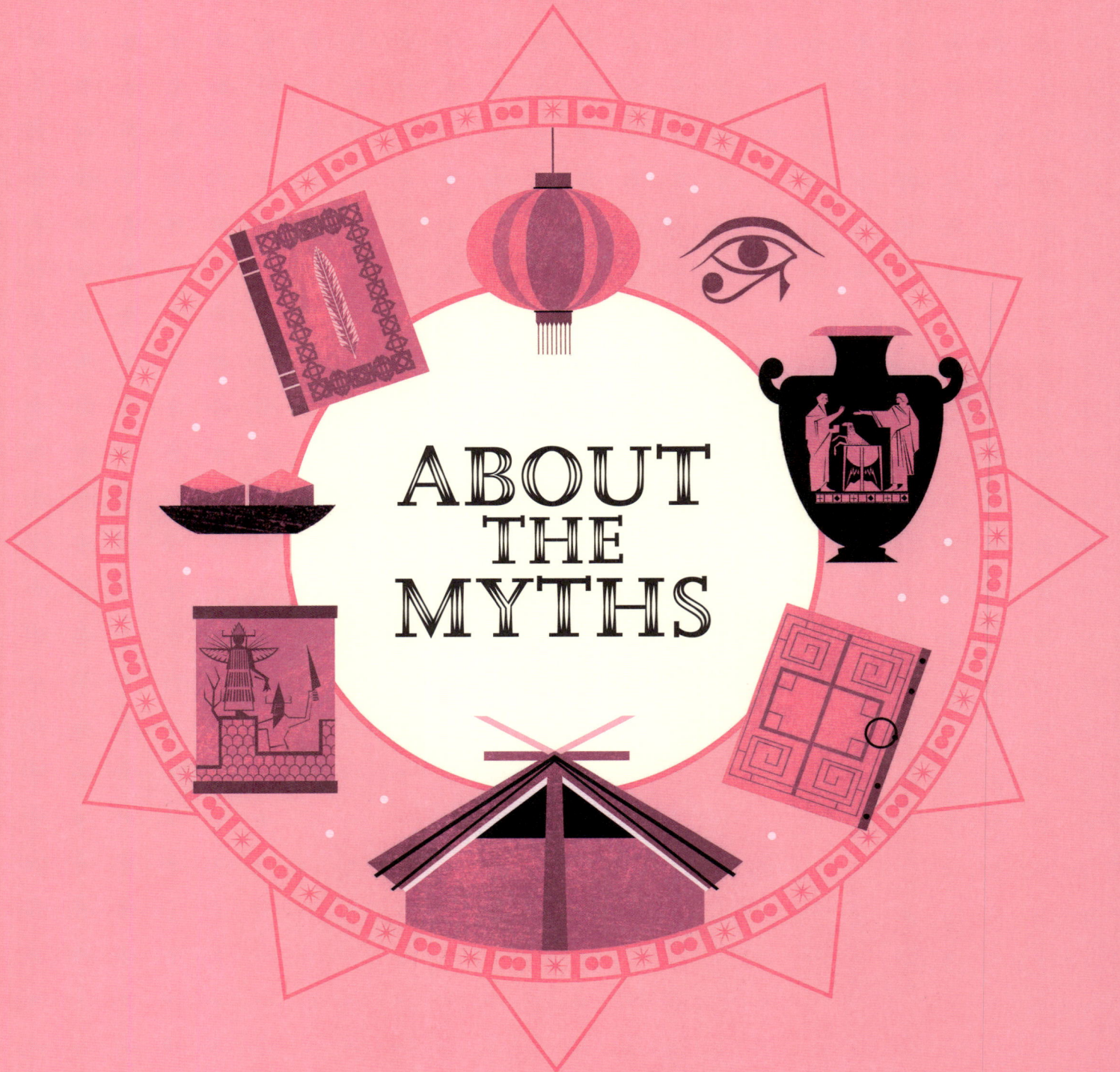

ABOUT THE MYTHS

Thanks to the people who have shared and continue to share the stories of goddesses, magical beings, and heroines, we are able to learn about them wherever and whenever they are from, even goddesses first worshipped thousands of years ago. There are many different ways in which the stories of these women have been preserved and continue to be told, from ancient books to modern festivals.

One of the most important ways in which different cultures share their stories is by speaking them. Communal spaces such as Māori wharenui, or meeting houses, allow them to be told to everyone.

People have painted and drawn stories for thousands of years. These images come in many forms, both for private homes and public spaces.

In northern Australia, in a cave now known as Rainbow Serpent Shelter, there is an ancient rock painting on the ceiling of the Rainbow Serpent. It measures more than 6 m (20 ft) long.

SHARING THE STORIES

The stories of goddesses and heroines have been retold for thousands of years. Whether by putting them to music, writing them down, or painting them, people have always found ways to pass these tales down the generations.

An illustrated scroll from 8th-century China shows the Chinese mother goddess Nüwa and her husband, the god Fuxi. It was made during a period known as the Tang Dynasty.

STATUES AND CARVINGS

Some artists work with stone and metal to create images of important figures. These pieces have the potential to survive for millennia and even today, ancient sculptures continue to be discovered.

The Vikings carved text and pictures into boulders to make runestones. A runestone from Tjängvide, Sweden, shows the hero Sigurd riding a horse and possibly Queen Grimhild or the warrior Brynhild.

Many ancient Egyptian statues depict the lion-headed goddess Sekhmet. More than 700 were created during the reign of Amenhotep III. They were located together and may have been displayed by a temple or lined a road.

OBJECTS

Images of goddesses and heroines are found on a variety of objects with both decorative and practical uses. Even everyday objects can tell us a lot about their stories.

Seals are used to leave impressions of images in wax or wet clay. Many ancient Mesopotamian seals are carved with images of the goddess Inanna, also known as Ishtar.

A carved stone altar from ancient Mexico shows a butterfly, one of the forms taken by the Aztec warrior goddess Itzpapalotl. Altars were used for offerings to the gods.

The ancient Greeks often painted scenes from mythology onto pots, called vases. One vase from the 5th century BCE shows Medea mixing a potion of youth for her husband Jason.

149

BOOKS AND SCROLLS

Over the years, people have written down the stories of goddesses and heroines. These books and scrolls have preserved important tales for future generations to read, although there are often many versions of each.

THE MABINOGION

The Mabinogion is the oldest collection of Welsh stories that survives. It was written down in two parts in the 13th and 14th centuries. Before this, tales, such as that of Rhiannon, would have been passed on by travelling storytellers.

THE NIHONGI

The Nihongi, or Japanese Chronicles, was finished in 720 CE and contains historical records of Japan and stories from Shinto religion, including that of the sun goddess Amaterasu.

THE SAMGUK YUSA

The Samguk Yusa is a collection of histories and stories from ancient Korea. It was put together by the Buddhist monk Il Yeon in the 13th century and contains the story of Ungnyeo.

THE PROSE EDDA

Written in the 13th century, The Prose Edda contains a huge number of stories about the gods and heroes of Norse mythology. It is partly based on a collection of poems known as The Poetic Edda.

THE MAHABHARATA

The Mahabharata is an ancient Indian epic poem written in Sanskrit. It is an important text in Hinduism and contains the tales of heroes and heroines, including Draupadi and the Pandava brothers.

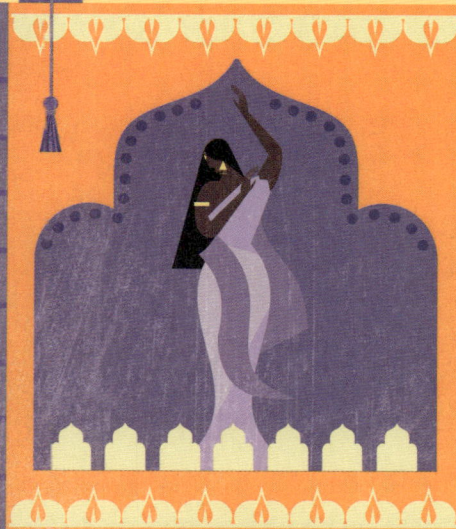

THE KALEVALA

The Kalevala is an epic poem written down by Elias Lönnrot in the 19th century. It tells the story of the creation of the world and the Finnish people.

THE BOOK OF THE DEAD

In ancient Egypt, it was common to create a "Book of the Dead" for the recently deceased containing spells for the afterlife. One example, known as the Papyrus of Ani, shows Hathor in her cow form.

THE THEOGONY

The Theogony is an Ancient Greek epic poem written by the poet Hesiod. It tells of the creation of the world and the story of how each generation of gods came to be, beginning with Gaia.

WORSHIPPING GODDESSES

Goddesses have been honoured for thousands of years in different ways, from the building of temples to the celebration of festivals. Although they come from different parts of the world and periods in time, they all have a role in their respective religions.

FESTIVALS

Festivals have always been an important way to thank different gods and ask them for their blessing. On these occasions, people typically come together to celebrate, share food, and make religious offerings.

The Mid-Autumn Festival is celebrated across China in autumn when the Moon is full. Offerings of food, including mooncakes, are put out for Chang'e, the goddess of the Moon.

Vasant Panchami is a festival held in honour of the Hindu goddess Saraswati. It celebrates the lead-up to spring and people often wear yellow clothing for it.

One of four ancient Irish festivals that celebrate the seasons, Imbolc traditionally marked the beginning of spring. At this time of year, ewes could begin to be milked and fires were lit to honour the goddess and expert dairywoman Brigid.

TEMPLES AND MONUMENTS

One of the most common ways that people celebrate their gods is to build impressive structures in their honour. These range from temples and shrines that serve as places of worship to huge monuments.

The Ishtar Gate was one of the grand arches that led into the ancient city of Babylon. It is decorated with animals, including lions that were the symbol of the goddess Ishtar, also called Inanna.

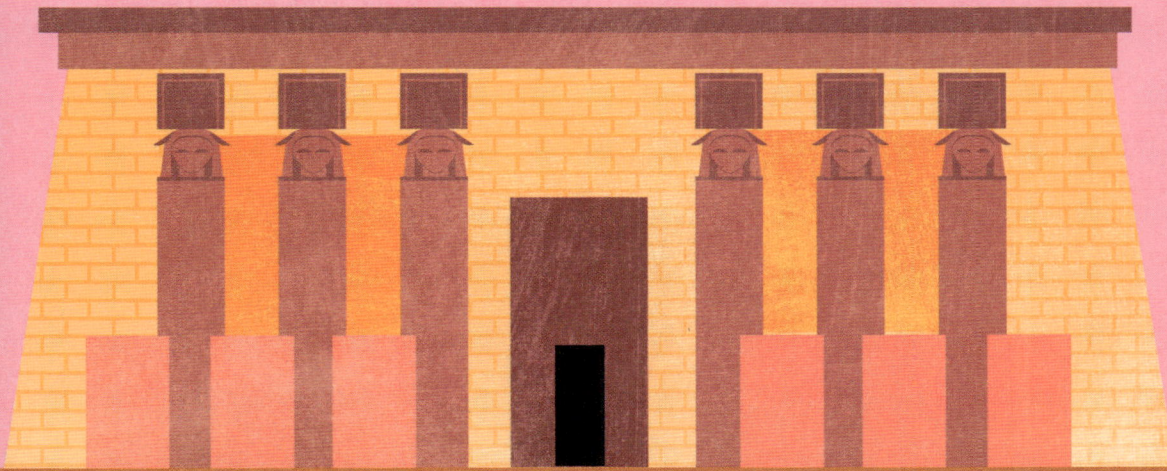

A famous temple dedicated to the ancient Egyptian goddess Hathor was built by the pharaoh Ptolemy XII around 2,000 years ago. It is part of a larger group of temples found near Dendera in modern Egypt.

The Ise Grand Shrine is located in the Japanese city of Ise. The Inner Shrine is dedicated to the sun goddess Amaterasu, an important deity in Shinto religion. The shrine is made from wood and is rebuilt every 20 years.

PRONUNCIATION GUIDE

ADLIVUN
AD-lee-vun

ADMETUS
ad-MEE-tuss

AEËTES
ai-EY-teez

AGNAR
AG-nar

ALCESTIS
al-SEST-iss

AME-NO-UZUME
a-MAY NO oo-ZOO-may

AMATERASU
a-ma-teh-RA-soo

AMENHOTEP
a-MEN-hoh-tep

ANAT
A-nat

ANI
A-nee

ANU
A-noo

APOLLO
a-POL-oh

ARACHNE
a-RAK-nee

ARGO
AR-go

ARJUNA
AR-joo-na

ASHERAH
A-sheh-ra

ASK
A-sk

ASU-SHU-NAMIR
a-SOO SHOO NA-meer

ATAEGINA
a-tai-GEE-na

ATALANTA
at-a-LAN-ta

ATHENA
ath-EE-na

ÂU CƠ
OH KHER

AXOMAMMA
AKS-oh-ma-ma

BAAL
BAYL

BABA YAGA
BA-ba ya-GA

BENZAITEN
ben-ZAI-ten

BHUMA
BOO-ma

BLODEUWEDD
blod-AI-weth

BOALIRI
BOH-a-li-ree

BRANGEIN
BRAN-geen

BRIGID
BRIH-jid

BRYNHILD
BREEN-hild

CAO
TSOW

CARDEA
KAR-dee-a

CHANG'E
CHAHNG-uh

CIGUAPA
sih-GWA-pa

CÚ CHULAINN
KOO HULL-en

DALI
DAH-lee

DANGUN WANGGEOM
TAN-guhn WAN-gom

DIDO
DAI-doh

DJINN
JIN

DRAUPADI
DROW-pa-dee

DRUPADA
DROO-pa-da

DUNYAZAD
DUN-ya-zad

DURYODHANA
du-ree-OH-da-na

DUSHASANA
DUSH-a-sa-na

EL
ELL

ELAINE OF ASTOLAT
eh-LAYN of A-stoh-lat

EMBLA
EM-blah

ENKI
ENG-kee

EPIMETHEUS
eh-pee-MEE-thee-uss

EPONA
eh-POH-na

ERATO
EH-ra-toh

ERESHKIGAL
eh-RESH-ki-gal

EROS
EER-oss

ERZULIE FRÉDA
ER-zoo-lee FREH-da

EVE
EEV

FAHAI
FAH-hai

FENGMENG
FUNG MUNG

FIONN
FIN

FREYA
FREY-yah

GAIA
GEY-a

GAWAINE
GA-wayn

GRIMHILD
GREEM-hild

GUDRUN
GUD-roon

GUNNAR
GUN-ar

GWAWL
GWOWL

HATHOR
HA-thor

HAUMIA-TIKITIKI
HOH-mee-a-TI-kee-TI-kee

HEPHAESTUS
heh-FEE-stuss

HERMES
HER-meez

HEROD ANTIPAS
HEH-rod AN-tee-pas

HESIOD
HESS-ee-od

HI'IAKA
HEE-ee-a-ka

HINEAHUONI
hih-nay-a-HOO-oh-nay

HODERI
HOH-de-ree

HOORI
HOH-or-ee

HOPOE
HOH-poh-ay

HOSUSERI
HOH-su-seh-ree

HWANUNG
HWA-nung

IARA
ee-AH-ra

IMBOLC
IM-bolk

INANNA
ih-NAH-na

ISHARA
ish-AH-ra

ISHTAR
ISH-tar

ISOLDE
IH-zol-duh

ITZPAPALOTL
ITS-pa-pa-lotl

JOLUNGGUL
YOH-lun-gul

KILAUEA
ki-la-WAY-a

KITSUNE
KIT-soo-nay

KONOHANA
KO-no-ha-na

KRISHNA
KRISH-na

KU-CHIN-DA-GAYYA
KOO CHIN DA GAI-a

LA MADREMONTE
LA ma-dreh-MON-tay

LADY BAI
LAY-dee BAI

LANCELOT
LAHN-sell-ot

LEHUA
LEH-hoo-a

LES LAVANDIÈRES
LEH la-von-dee-AIR

LI
LEE

LILITH
LIH-lith

LIRIOPE lee-ree-OHP-ee	**NERGAL** NER-gal	**QUEEN OF SHEBA** SHEE-ba	**TLAZOLTEOTL** tla-zol-tay-OH-tel
LLEU LLAW HLEY HLOW	**NGANU LEIMA** n-GA-noo LAY-ma	**RA** RAR	**TRISTAN** TRIH-stan
LOHI'AU LOH-hee-ow	**NINIGI** NI-ni-gee	**RANGINUI** RANG-i-noo-ee	**TSUNEMASA** TSOO-ne-ma-sa
LOUHI LOH-ee	**NÜWA** NYOO-wa	**RAYMOND** RAY-mond	**TŪMATAUENGA** TOO-ma-tow-eng-a
LUNA LOO-na	**OBATALA** oh-BA-ta-la	**RHIANNON** rhee-A-non	**TUATHA DÉ DANANN** TOO-ha DAY DAH-nan
LUTZELFRAU LOOTZ-el-frow	**ODIN** OH-din	**RONGO-MĀ-TĀNE** RONG-o-MA-TAH-nay	**TUONETAR** TOO-oh-neh-tar
MABINOGION ma-bih-NO-gee-on	**OHOYAMATSUMI** o-ho-YA-mat-soo-mee	**SADHBH** SAHV	**TUONI** TOO-oh-nee
MAHUIKA MA-hoo-ee-ka	**OÍSIN** OH-sheen	**SAHADEVA** SA-ha-day-va	**UNGNYEO** UNG-yo
MAMAN BRIGITTE MA-mon BRI-jeet	**OLOKUN** o-LO-kun	**SALOME** sa-LOH-mee	**URDUJA** er-DOO-ha
MAMAN DLO MA-mon DLOH	**OLYMPUS** oh-LIMP-uss	**SARASWATI** SA-ra-swa-tee	**USHAS** OO-shass
MARI ma-REE	**ORUNMILA** o-ROON-mill-a	**SAULE** SOW-lay	**VÄINÄMÖINEN** VAI-na-moy-nen
MĀUI MOW-ee	**OYA** oi-YA	**SCÁTHACH** SKA-hahk	**VALKYRIE** VAL-ki-ree
MAZU MA-zoo	**PACHAMAMA** PA-cha-ma-ma	**SEDNA** SED-na	**VASILISA** va-sih-LEE-sa
MEDEA meh-DEE-a	**PANA'EWA** pa-na-AY-va	**SEKHMET** SEK-met	**VIKARNA** VI-kar-na
MEDEINA meh-DEE-na	**PANDAVA** PAN-da-va	**SELKIE** SEL-kee	**WAIMARIWI** WAI-ma-ri-wee
MELUSINE MEL-yoo-seen	**PANDORA** pan-DOR-a	**SHAHRAZAD** sha-ha-ra-ZAD	**WAWALAG** WA-wa-lag
MENESS MEH-ness	**PANIA** PAH-nee-a	**SHAHRYAR** SHA-ree-ah	**WHUPPITY STOORIE** WUP-it-ee STOO-ree
MENGJIAO MUNG-jee-ow	**PAPATŪĀNUKU** pa-pa-too-a-NOO-koo	**SHTRIGË** SHTREE-g	**XIWANGMU** SHEE-wahng-moo
MEPISA MEH-pee-sa	**PAU-O-PALAE** POW-O-PA-lai	**SIGRID** SIG-reed	**XU XIAN** SHU SHEN
MOREMORE MOR-ey-MOR-ey	**PELE** PEH-lay	**SIGURD** SIG-urd	**YAM** YAM
MORGANA mor-GAH-na	**PERSEPHONE** per-SEF-oh-nee	**SIM CHEONG** SHIM CHONG	**YI** YEE
MULAN MOO-lan	**PINCOYA** pin-KOI-ya	**SUSANOO** soo-sa-NO	**YUDHISHTHIRA** yud-ISH-thih-ra
NAIAD NAI-ad	**PRESSINA** press-EE-na	**TĀNE-MAHUTA** TAH-nay-MA-hoo-ta	**ZEUS** ZYOOS
NAKULA NA-koo-la	**PROMETHEUS** pro-MEE-thee-uss	**MORRIGÁN** mor-i-GAHN	**ZIGU** ZI-goo
NAMTAR NAM-tar	**PTOLEMY** TO-leh-mee	**TI JEANNE** TEE ZHON	**ZIXU** ZI-shoo
NARCISSUS nar-SISS-uss	**PWYLL** POILHL	**TITAN** TAI-tan	

GLOSSARY

AKKADIAN relating to an ancient group of people who lived in Mesopotamia

AMORITES ancient people who lived in the area of Syria and southern Mesopotamia in modern-day Iraq

ANCIENT EGYPT civilization that existed in and around modern-day Egypt from about 3100 BCE to 30 BCE

ANCIENT GREECE civilization composed of various city states that occupied modern-day Greece from about 1200 BCE to 600 CE

ANCIENT ROME civilization that existed from about 700 BCE to 400 CE, with its capital in Rome

APPRENTICE someone who is training under an expert in a specific field

ARTHURIAN time period when the legendary King Arthur ruled the Celtic Britons

AZTEC relating to a people that lived in Mexico from the 14th to the 16th century

BABYLON capital city of the ancient Babylonian Empire, located in Mesopotamia

BALTIC certain countries with a coast on the Baltic Sea, including Estonia, Latvia, and Lithuania

BASQUE relating to a people that live in parts of northern Spain and western France

BIWA Japanese string instrument similar to a lute, traditionally played during storytelling

BURGUNDY region of France that until the 9th century was an independent kingdom

CARTHAGE ancient city that grew into an empire, located in modern-day Tunisia

CELTIC relating to groups of people from various parts of Europe from around 800 BCE to 50 BCE who shared a language

CHANUPA sacred ceremonial pipe used by the Lakota people

CHARIOT wheeled vehicle usually pulled by horses, but also some other animals

CHEROKEE one of the largest groups of the Indigenous People of North America

CHRISTIANITY one of the largest religions in the world, originating in the Middle East

COLCHIS country from ancient Greek myth, found by the Black Sea

DJINN type of spirit that can change shape

DRUID Celtic religious leader with powers given to them by the gods

ELIXIR potion used for magical or medicinal purposes

FAIRY magical creature that looks different in many cultures, but is most often small and winged

FLAX flowering plant with long, pointed leaves

GAULISH relating to a group of ancient people who lived in western Europe

GODDESS female deity worshipped by followers of a certain religion

HAUSA relating to a group of people who live mainly in West Africa

HINDUISM one of the largest religions in the world, originating in India

HURRIAN relating to a group of ancient people who lived in Asia

IBERIAN relating to a group of ancient people who lived in the Iberian Peninsula in southwest Europe

IMMORTALITY power that means an individual will never die

INCA relating to a people who lived in North and South America from the 13th to the 16th century

INDRAPRASTHA capital city of the Pandava brothers' kingdom

INUIT name used for various Indigenous peoples who live in the Arctic and subarctic regions of North America

ISLAM one of the largest religions in the world, originating in the Middle East

JOUSTING medieval sport where two competitors aim poles, called lances, at one another while riding horses

JUDAISM one of the oldest religions in the world, which originated in the Middle East

KAYLUKARI legendary kingdom in Southeast Asia ruled by the warrior princess Urduja

KINGDOM OF ISRAEL ancient kingdom found on the eastern shore of the Mediterranean, referenced in the Hebrew Bible

LAKOTA one of the groups of the Indigenous People of North America

LOOM hand-operated machine used to weave tapestries

LWA divine spirits worshipped in the Vodou religion of Haiti

MĀORI relating to a people from New Zealand and the Cook Islands

MEITEI relating to a people from Manipur in northeast India

MERMAID mythical creature with the upper body of a woman and the tail of a fish

MESOPOTAMIA ancient region in western Asia found in modern-day Iraq

MOONCAKE round pastry from China with various fillings

MORTAL human

MUSE any one of a group of nine ancient Greek goddesses responsible for inspiring different kinds of art

NAIAD nymph in ancient Greek mythology who protects bodies of fresh water

NEW TESTAMENT second of the two books that make up the Christian Bible

NORSE relating to a people who lived in Scandinavia between the 8th and 11th centuries, also known as Vikings

OCHRE natural pigment made up of sand and clay

ORISHA divine spirit worshipped in Yoruba religion

ORKNEY ISLANDS group of islands off the northern coast of Scotland

PHARAOH ancient Egyptian king or queen

PHERAE oldest city in Thessaly, which was a region of ancient Greece

POHJOLA legendary kingdom north of Finland

SANSKRIT ancient language from southern Asia that is used for sacred Hindu texts

SHEBA ancient kingdom mentioned in both the Hebrew Bible and the Quran

SHINTOISM religion originating in Japan

SLAVIC relating to a group of peoples from eastern Europe who speak related languages

SUMERIAN relating to an ancient group of people who lived in Sumer, one of the earliest known civilizations in Mesopotamia

TUATHA DÉ DANAAN family of magical beings in Irish mythology, sometimes known as fairies or gods

UNDERWORLD land where human souls go after they die according to numerous religions

VALKYRIE group of women in Norse mythology who guide the souls of dead warriors to the afterlife

VEENA stringed instrument from India

VIZIER title given to important court officials in ancient Egypt and parts of Asia

WITCH magical person, usually a woman, who can cast spells and brew magical potions

YORUBA relating to a group of people who live in West Africa

INDEX

DK | Penguin Random House

Written by Dr Jean Menzies
Illustrated by Katie Ponder

Project editor Olivia Stanford
Designer Bettina Myklebust Støvne
Editorial assistant Kieran Jones

Managing editor Jonathan Melmoth
Managing art editor Diane Peyton Jones
Senior production editor Nikoleta Parasaki
Senior production controller Inderjit Bhullar
Publishing director Sarah Larter

First published in Great Britain in 2023 by
Dorling Kindersley Limited
DK, One Embassy Gardens, 8 Viaduct Gardens,
London, SW11 7BW

The authorised representative in the EEA is
Dorling Kindersley Verlag GmbH. Arnulfstr. 124,
80636 Munich, Germany

Text copyright © Jean Menzies 2023
Illustration © Katie Ponder 2023
Copyright © 2023 Dorling Kindersley Limited
A Penguin Random House Company
10 9 8 7 6 5 4 3 2 1
001-334693-Jul/2023

A CIP catalogue record for this book
is available from the British Library.
ISBN: 978-0-2416-0977-4

Printed and bound in China

For the curious
www.dk.com

FSC
MIX
Paper | Supporting
responsible forestry
FSC™ C018179

This book was made with Forest
Stewardship Council™ certified
paper - one small step in DK's
commitment to a sustainable future.
For more information go to
www.dk.com/our-green-pledge

The publisher would like to thank the following people
for their assistance in the preparation of this book:
Abi Maxwell for editorial assistance; Caroline Hunt
for proofreading; and Helen Peters for the index.

ABOUT THE AUTHOR

Dr Jean Menzies runs a podcast
about classics and mythology, and
has a YouTube channel, where she
discusses literature and history.
She has spoken about ancient
Greece to audiences of all ages,
and holds a PhD in women in
classical Athens.

ABOUT THE ILLUSTRATOR

Katie Ponder is an award-winning
illustrator whose work has been
featured in exhibitions at Somerset
House, and the DK books *Greek Myths,
Norse Myths, and Egyptian Myths.*
Her inspirations include ballet,
ghost stories, and the greenhouses
at Kew Gardens.

CONSULTANTS

- Professor Miranda Aldhouse-Green
- Professor Ginetta Candelario
- Dr Heide Crawford
- Professor Victor Friedman
- Assistant Professor Ziortza Gandarias Beldarrain
- Dr Amy Fuller
- Dr Ragnhild Ljosland
- Dr Veronica Muskheli
- Dr Georgia Petridou
- Dr Quang Phu Van
- Professor Joyce Tyldesley
- Professor Tammi Schneider
- Associate Professor Hilary-Joy Virtanen

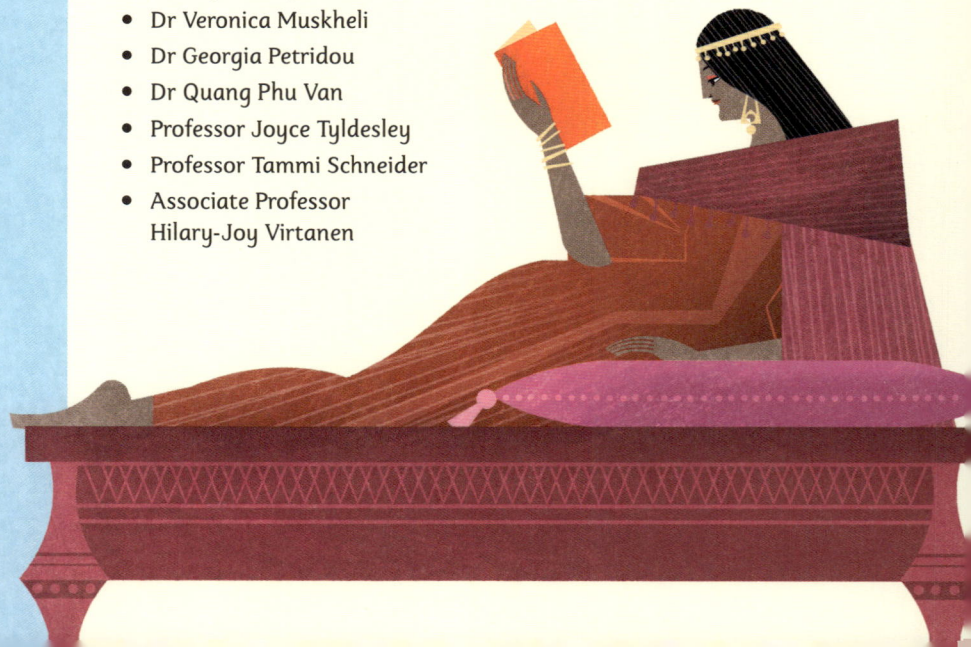